HAMLYN
ALL COLOUR
ENTERTAINING

HAMLYN ALL COLOUR ENTERTAINING

HAMLYN

Front cover shows, left to right:
Vine Leaf and Fish Mousses (recipe 1), Traditional
Roast Beef (recipe 129), Cassata alla Siciliana (recipe 213).

Back cover shows, clockwise from top left:
Iced Tomato and Basil Soup (recipe 53), Angels on
Horseback (recipe 241), Open Sandwiches (recipe 161),
Chipolata Kebabs (recipe 189),
Barbecued Boned Leg of Lamb (recipe 89).

First published 1991
Hamlyn is an imprint of Octopus Illustrated Publishing
Michelin House, 81 Fulham Road, London SW3 6RB
part of Reed International Books Limited

A catalogue record of this book is available
from the British Library

ISBN 0 600 57420 2

Produced by Mandarin Offset
Printed in Hong Kong

OTHER TITLES IN THIS SERIES INCLUDE

Hamlyn All Colour Cookbook
Hamlyn New All Colour Cookbook
Hamlyn All Colour Microwave Cookbook
Hamlyn All Colour Quick and Easy Cookbook
Hamlyn All Colour Vegetarian Cookbook
Hamlyn All Colour Oriental Cookbook
Hamlyn All Colour Cakes and Baking
Hamlyn All Colour Puddings and Desserts
Hamlyn All Colour Slimming Cookbook
Best of Hamlyn All Colour Cooking

CONTENTS

USEFUL FACTS AND FIGURES

NOTES ON METRICATION
In this book quantities are given in metric and Imperial measures. Exact conversion from Imperial to metric measures does not usually give very convenient working quantities and so the metric measures have been rounded off into units of 25 grams. The table below shows the recommended equivalents.

Ounces	Approx g to nearest whole figure	Recommended conversion to nearest unit of 25	Ounces	Approx g to nearest whole figure	Recommended conversion to nearest unit of 25
1	28	25	9	255	250
2	57	50	10	283	275
3	85	75	11	312	300
4	113	100	12	340	350
5	142	150	13	368	375
6	170	175	14	396	400
7	198	200	15	425	425
8	227	225	16(1lb)	454	450

Note
When converting quantities over 16 oz first add the appropriate figures in the centre column, then adjust to the nearest unit of 25. As a general guide, 1 kg (1000 g) equals 2.2 lb or about 2 lb 3 oz. This method of conversion gives good results in nearly all cases, although in certain pastry and cake recipes a more accurate conversion is necessary to produce a balanced recipe.

Liquid measures
The millilitre has been used in this book and the following table gives a few examples.

Imperial	Approx ml to nearest whole figure	Recommended ml	Imperial	Approx ml to nearest whole figure	Recommended ml
¼	142	150 ml	1 pint	567	600 ml
½	283	300 ml	1½ pints	851	900 ml
¾	425	450 ml	1¾ pints	992	1000 ml (1 litre)

Spoon measures
All spoon measures given in this book are level unless otherwise stated.

Can sizes
At present, cans are marked with the exact (usually to the nearest whole number) metric equivalent of the Imperial weight of the contents, so we have followed this practice when giving can sizes.

Oven temperatures
The table below gives recommended equivalents.

	°C	°F	Gas Mark		°C	°F	Gas Mark
Very cool	110	225	¼	Moderately hot	190	375	5
	120	250	½		200	400	6
Cool	140	275	1	Hot	220	425	7
	150	300	2		230	450	8
Moderate	160	325	3	Very hot	240	475	9
	180	350	4				

NOTES FOR AMERICAN AND AUSTRALIAN USERS
In America the 8-fl oz measuring cup is used. In Australia metric measures are now used in conjunction with the standard 250-ml measuring cup. The Imperial pint, used in Britain and Australia, is 20 fl oz, while the American pint is 16 fl oz. It is important to remember that the Australian tablespoon differs from both the British and American tablespoons; the table below gives a comparison. The British standard tablespoon, which has been used throughout this book, holds 17.7 ml, the American 14.2 ml, and the Australian 20 ml. A teaspoon holds approximately 5 ml in all three countries.

British	American	Australian
1 teaspoon	1 teaspoon	1 teaspoon
1 tablespoon	1 tablespoon	1 tablespoon
2 tablespoons	3 tablespoons	2 tablespoons
3½ tablespoons	4 tablespoons	3 tablespoons
4 tablespoons	5 tablespoons	3½ tablespoons

AN IMPERIAL/AMERICAN GUIDE TO SOLID AND LIQUID MEASURES

Imperial	American	Imperial	American
Solid measures		**Liquid measures**	
1 lb butter or margarine	2 cups	¼ pint liquid	⅔ cup liquid
1 lb flour	4 cups	½ pint	1¼ cups
1 lb granulated or caster sugar	2 cups	¾ pint	2 cups
1 lb icing sugar	3 cups	1 pint	2½ cups
8 oz rice	1 cup	1½ pints	3¾ cups
		2 pints	5 cups (2½ pints)

NOTE: WHEN MAKING ANY OF THE RECIPES IN THIS BOOK, ONLY FOLLOW ONE SET OF MEASURES AS THEY ARE NOT INTERCHANGEABLE.

INTRODUCTION

Entertaining people, whether friends, relatives or business colleagues, almost always involves serving food and drink. With HAMLYN ALL COLOUR ENTERTAINING to hand, nothing could be easier.

Here are over 250 recipes, written clearly and simply so that even inexperienced cooks may use them with confidence. Each recipe has a full-colour photograph to show how the finished dish looks and to offer decorative and serving hints, and a calorie count to help in planning well-balanced meals. Cook's Tips at the end of the recipes provide additional information, including serving suggestions, alternative ingredients and useful information on cooking techniques.

The recipes have been carefully chosen to provide a good range of dishes suitable for many sorts of occasion, from the formal elegance of dinner parties for just a few people to the fun of informal backyard barbecues and teenagers' disco parties. They are gathered into chapters which make it quick and easy to find the right recipes or ideas to suit the occasion being planned. Look in Coffee and Tea Parties for biscuits and cakes to serve at fund-raising coffee mornings, and in Cocktail Parties for those delicious little nibbles and finger foods, plus a few cocktails, that help make the talk flow easily at early-evening drinks parties. In Special Occasions will be found a good selection of traditional dishes, like Roast Beef and Christmas Pudding, as well as dishes for those really important occasions like summer weddings and christening parties. Toddlers and teenagers alike are catered for in the chapter of recipes for parties for the young, while Supper Parties should provide plenty of inspiration for dishes to be prepared quickly or well in advance for those after-theatre meals. The Outdoor Meals chapter offers recipes for barbecues, picnics or occasions like bonfire night parties, and in Buffet Parties can be found many ideas for fork suppers and stand-up parties.

As well as this exciting collection of recipes, HAMLYN ALL COLOUR ENTERTAINING has an impressive collection of extra information, with the accent on relaxed entertaining. The special Party Planning section at the end of the book has lots of good advice on advance planning, notes on calculating the amounts of basic ingredients and drinks needed for different kinds of occasion, notes on serving and storing wines and other drinks, and a chart of the wines which go best with different types of food.

There is also a page of menu suggestions for occasions ranging from a supper party and a vegetarian lunch for just four people to a buffet party and a cocktail party for thirty guests.

All in all, there is plenty to inspire everyone to start entertaining – now!

FORMAL MEALS

Dinner and lunch parties, with guests gathered round an elegantly laid table, allow the well-prepared cook to shine. To help things go smoothly, choose from among the recipes here first and last courses which may be prepared well in advance of the meal.

1 VINE LEAF AND FISH MOUSSES

Preparation time:
30 minutes, plus chilling

Cooking time:
40 minutes

Oven temperature:
160 C, 325 F, gas 3

Serves 8

Calories:
258 per portion

YOU WILL NEED:
approx 100 g/4 oz vine leaves in brine (canned or in packets)
100 g/4 oz smoked salmon
1 kg/2 lb plaice fillets, skinned
4 eggs
3 tablespoons dry white wine
5 tablespoons double cream
1 teaspoon lemon juice
salt and pepper
pinch of ground coriander
lemon slices, to garnish

Rinse the vine leaves in water to remove excess brine. Drain well. Lightly grease 8 ramekin dishes and line the inside of each with a double layer of vine leaves. Cut the salmon into strips and roll into 8 larger and 8 smaller rolls.

Purée or liquidize the plaice and beat in the eggs, followed by the wine, cream, lemon juice, salt and pepper and coriander. Put a spoonful of the fish mixture into each ramekin, place one of the larger smoked salmon rolls on each and cover with the remaining purée.

Stand the ramekins in a roasting tin with water to come at least halfway up the sides of the dishes. Cover with foil and cook in a preheated oven for about 40 minutes or until set and cooked through.

Leave to cool, then chill. Turn out carefully and serve each one topped with a smoked salmon roll and a lemon slice. Serve with thinly sliced brown bread and butter.

■ COOK'S TIP

If preferred, the mousses may be served warm rather than chilled. In this case, leave them to stand for 10 minutes before turning out and serve at once.

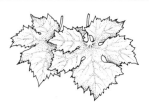

2 LEEKS IN PASTRY CASES

Preparation time:
15 minutes

Cooking time:
20 minutes

Oven temperature:
220 C, 425 F, gas 7

Serves 4

Calories:
688 per portion

YOU WILL NEED:
1 × 375 g/13 oz pack frozen puff pastry, thawed
1 egg, beaten
50 g/2 oz butter
350 g/12 oz white part of leeks, thinly sliced
juice of ½ lemon
salt and pepper
150 ml/¼ pint double cream
4 sprigs parsley, to garnish

Roll out the pastry to a rectangle 26 × 15 cm/10 × 6 inches. Cut into 4 pieces, each 13 × 7½ cm/5 × 3 inches. Score each piece lightly in a diamond pattern and brush the tops with beaten egg. Place on a wetted baking sheet and bake in a preheated oven for 20 minutes.

Meanwhile, prepare the filling. Melt the butter in a pan, add the leeks and cook gently for about 10 minutes until soft but not browned. Add the lemon juice, salt and pepper to the leeks, stir well, then add the cream. Bring to the boil, stirring constantly. Cook for 2-3 minutes.

When the pastry slices are cooked, remove from the oven and cut each one in half horizontally. Divide the leek mixture between the bottom halves of the pastry slices, then replace the pastry top. Serve immediately, garnished with parsley sprigs.

■ COOK'S TIP

Put the pastry into a thoroughly pre-heated oven to ensure it rises evenly and cooks in beautifully light and flaky layers.

3 TERRINE DE CANARD

Preparation time:
20 minutes, plus
chilling overnight

Cooking time:
1½-1¾ hours

Oven temperature:
180 C, 350 F, gas 4

Serves 8

Calories:
490 per portion

YOU WILL NEED:
1 × 1.5 kg/3 lb oven-ready duck, skin
  and bones removed
450 g/1 lb minced pork
350 g/12 oz minced veal
1 garlic clove, crushed (see Cook's
  Tip)
1 tablespoon Worcestershire sauce
juice of 1 orange
2 teaspoons dried mixed herbs
150 ml/¼ pint dry red wine
salt and pepper
10 rashers rindless streaky bacon
1 tablespoon brandy
FOR THE GARNISH
orange twists
watercress sprigs

Dice the duck meat and mix with the pork and veal. Add the garlic, Worcestershire sauce, orange juice, herbs, wine, and salt and pepper to taste. Cover and chill overnight.

Using a sharp knife, stretch the bacon rashers and use to line the base and sides of a 1 kg/2 lb terrine or loaf tin. Press the meat mixture into the tin, sprinkle with the brandy and cover with foil. Place in a roasting pan and pour in enough boiling water to come halfway up the sides of the pan. Cook in a preheated oven for 1½-1¾ hours.

Leave until cold then turn out. Garnish the terrine with orange twists (see recipe 14) and watercress.

▨ COOK'S TIP

If you do not have a garlic press, peeled garlic may be easily crushed by pressing it under the flat blade of a large knife.

4 THREE-COLOUR TERRINE

Preparation time:
15-20 minutes, plus
cooling

Cooking time:
1 hour

Oven temperature:
160 C, 325 F, gas 3

Serves 6

Calories:
203 per portion

YOU WILL NEED:
100 g/4 oz cooked chicken
350 g/12 oz skimmed milk soft cheese
3 eggs
salt and white pepper
100 g/4 oz spinach, cooked
100 g/4 oz carrots, cooked
FOR THE SAUCE
6-8 spring onions, chopped
2 tablespoons oil
450 g/1 lb tomatoes, skinned and
  chopped
juice of 1 orange
1 tablespoon tomato purée

Place the chicken, one third of the cheese and one egg in an electric blender or food processor and work to a purée. Season with salt and pepper to taste. Repeat this process twice, using the spinach, then the carrots, in place of the chicken.

Grease a 450 g/1 lb loaf tin and spoon in the chicken mixture. Carefully spoon over the carrot mixture, then the spinach mixture. Place the tin in a roasting pan half-filled with water and cook in a preheated oven for 1 hour.

Meanwhile make the sauce. Fry the spring onions gently in 1 tablespoon of the oil for 2 minutes. Drain. Process the onions and remaining ingredients together in a blender until combined well. Season to taste.

When the terrine is cool turn it out on to a serving plate and surround with the sauce.

▨ COOK'S TIP

The tomato and orange sauce recipe here makes about 450 ml/¾ pint, and is very good served with fried fish.

5 CREAM OF CARROT AND DILL SOUP

Preparation time:
25 minutes

Cooking time:
45 minutes

Serves 8

Calories:
98 per portion

YOU WILL NEED:
50 g/2 oz butter or margarine
1 onion, chopped
450 g/1 lb carrots, diced
100 g/4 oz peeled potatoes, diced
900 ml/1½ pints chicken stock
2 tablespoons lemon juice
salt and pepper
good pinch of ground coriander
150 ml/¼ pint unsweetened orange juice
300-450 ml/½-¾ pint milk or skimmed milk or part milk and part single cream
2 tablespoons chopped fresh dill

Melt the fat in a pan, add the onion and fry gently until it begins to soften. Add the carrots and potato and continue frying for 4-5 minutes, without allowing the vegetables to colour, stirring occasionally. Add the stock, lemon juice, salt, pepper and coriander and bring to the boil. Cover the pan and simmer gently for 30 minutes until tender.

Cool slightly, then purée, liquidize or sieve the soup and return it to a clean pan with the orange juice and 300 ml/½ pint of the milk.

Bring the soup back to the boil and add the dill and sufficient extra milk to give the desired consistency. Simmer for 2-3 minutes then adjust the seasonings and serve.

■ COOK'S TIP

This soup may be frozen for up to 3 months. Freeze it when the orange juice and 300 ml/½ pint of milk have been added but not the dill or extra milk.

6 SUMMER VEGETABLE SOUP

Preparation time:
10 minutes, plus chilling

Serves 6

Calories:
166 per portion

YOU WILL NEED:
8 large ripe tomatoes
2 garlic cloves
½ small onion
½ cucumber
1 green pepper, cored and seeded
1 red pepper, cored and seeded
1 thyme sprig
2 parsley sprigs
6 tablespoons olive oil
4 tablespoons lemon juice
600 ml/1 pint tomato juice, chilled
few drops of Tabasco sauce
FOR THE GARNISH
garlic-flavoured croûtons (see Cook's Tip)

Chop the tomatoes, garlic, onion, cucumber and peppers roughly. Put these ingredients into an electric blender and blend until smooth. Add the herbs and blend again.

Strain into a bowl and chill for several hours.

Just before serving, mix the olive oil and lemon juice together. Add the tomato juice and Tabasco, and gradually stir this mixture into the soup. Garnish with the croûtons and serve black olives and capers as accompaniments.

■ COOK'S TIP

For garlic-flavoured croûtons, heat 1 or 2 chopped garlic cloves in oil, removing the garlic with a slotted spoon before adding the cubes of day-old bread *for the croûtons. Drain the crisp and golden croûtons on absorbent kitchen paper.*

7   WATERCRESS AND CUCUMBER SOUP

Preparation time: 15 minutes	YOU WILL NEED: *1 small onion, chopped*
	½ cucumber, diced
Cooking time: 35 minutes	*600 ml/1 pint chicken stock*
	1 bunch watercress
Serves 4	*2 teaspoons lemon juice*
	salt and pepper
Calories: 43 per portion	*good pinch of ground coriander*
	300 ml/½ pint milk
	2 teaspoons cornflour

Put the onion, cucumber and stock into a saucepan and bring to the boil. Cover and simmer for 15 minutes.

Reserve a few sprigs of watercress for garnish and chop the remainder. Add the chopped watercress, lemon juice, salt and pepper and coriander to the saucepan, cover and simmer for a further 10 minutes.

Cool slightly, then purée, liquidize or sieve the soup. Return to a clean pan, add the milk and bring back to the boil.

Blend the cornflour with a little cold water, add to the soup and bring back to the boil again. Simmer for 2 minutes, then adjust the seasonings. Serve garnished with the reserved watercress sprigs.

8   PRAWN PATE

Preparation time: 5 minutes, plus chilling	YOU WILL NEED: *100 g/4 oz butter*
	1 garlic clove, crushed
	1 teaspoon crushed coriander seeds
Cooking time: 6-7 minutes	*100 g/4 oz peeled prawns, thawed (if frozen)*
Serves 4	*3 tablespoons double or whipping cream*
Calories: 275 per portion	*salt*
	cayenne pepper
	FOR THE GARNISH
	lemon wedges
	sprigs of parsley

Melt the butter in a heavy frying pan over a low heat, then add the garlic and coriander and fry gently for 2-3 minutes. Add the prawns and turn to coat with the butter.

Transfer the contents of the pan to a food processor or electric blender and process until smooth. Add the cream and process again briefly. Season to taste with salt and cayenne pepper.

Spoon the prawn pâté into individual pots and chill. Serve garnished with lemon wedges and sprigs of parsley.

▦ COOK'S TIP

This soup is also good served cold as a summer-time first course. Make it the day or morning before it is to be served and keep it covered in the refrigerator.

▦ COOK'S TIP

This easy pâté may be made the day before it is to be served and kept, covered, in the refrigerator. Serve it with freshly made toast.

9 CRISPY MUSHROOMS WITH HERB SAUCE

Preparation time:
15 minutes

Cooking time:
about 15 minutes

Serves 6

Calories:
282 per portion

YOU WILL NEED:
450 g/1 lb button mushrooms
oil for deep frying
FOR THE BATTER
100 g/4 oz plain flour
pinch of salt
1 tablespoon oil
150 ml/¼ pint water
2 egg whites
FOR THE SAUCE
8 tablespoons mayonnaise
2 garlic cloves, crushed
2 tablespoons chopped parsley
1 tablespoon chopped basil

First, make the batter. Sift the flour and salt into a bowl, then gradually beat in the oil and water. Whisk the egg whites until very stiff, then fold into the batter.

Drop the mushrooms into the batter. Heat the oil in a deep-fryer to 190 C/375 F. Deep-fry the mushrooms in batches, lifting them from the batter to the oil, using a slotted spoon. Drain on absorbent kitchen paper and keep hot while frying the remaining mushrooms.

Mix the sauce ingredients together and spoon into a bowl. Serve immediately, with the hot mushrooms.

10 PARMA HAM WITH AVOCADO

Preparation time:
10 minutes

Serves 2

Calories:
385 per portion

YOU WILL NEED:
1 ripe medium avocado
6 slices Parma ham, about 75 g/3 oz
* total weight*
FOR THE DRESSING
1 tablespoon olive oil
1 teaspoon lemon juice
1 garlic clove, crushed
2 teaspoons fresh chopped parsley
salt and pepper

Cut the avocado in half and remove the stone. Peel off the skin and cut each half into 3 thick slices.

Wrap each slice of ham around a slice of avocado. Arrange on a serving dish or individual dishes.

Place all the dressing ingredients in a screw-topped jar and shake well to mix together.

Pour the dressing over to serve.

■ COOK'S TIP

Use fresh herbs, rather than dried, for better flavour and texture. If liked, fresh thyme, oregano or tarragon could be used in place of the basil in the sauce.

■ COOK'S TIP

For an unusual variation use fresh figs instead of the avocado. Allow 2 ripe figs per person and cut each down through the centre in a cross. Arrange the figs on *the ham and omit the dressing. Sprinkle with black pepper, if liked.*

11 TARAMASALATA

Preparation time:
20 minutes

Serves 4

Calories:
435 per portion

YOU WILL NEED:
4 large slices white bread, crusts
    removed
6 tablespoons cold water
100 g/4 oz skinned smoked cod's roe
    or salted tarama (grey mullet's roe)
1 large garlic clove, crushed
3 tablespoons lemon juice
freshly ground black pepper
150 ml/¼ pint olive oil
FOR THE GARNISH
black olives
sprigs of parsley

Soak the bread in the cold water for 10 minutes, and then squeeze it lightly, without leaving it too dry.

Put the bread into a liquidizer or food processor with the cod's roe or tarama, garlic, lemon juice and black pepper to taste. Blend to a smooth paste.

Gradually add the olive oil, as for mayonnaise, blending the mixture thoroughly after each addition.

Serve the prepared taramasalata garnished with black olives and sprigs of parsley.

12 STUFFED PEAR HORS D'OEUVRE

Preparation time:
10 minutes

Serves 4

Calories:
248 per portion

YOU WILL NEED:
100 g/4 oz cream cheese
1 tablespoon chopped chives
2 teaspoons chopped parsley
25 g/1 oz walnuts, chopped
1 apple, peeled, cored and grated
2 teaspoons lemon juice
1 head of chicory
4 large ripe pears
4 slices Parma ham

Beat the cream cheese until soft. Mix in the herbs and nuts, then fold in the apple and lemon juice.

Arrange the chicory leaves on 4 individual serving plates. Peel the pears, halve and remove the cores. Spoon the filling into the core cavities and arrange two halves on each plate.

Roll up the ham slices and place in the centre. Serve immediately.

■ COOK'S TIP

This well-known Greek dish is traditionally served with pitta bread, sold in most supermarkets. Warm the pitta bread before serving it.

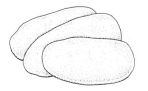

■ COOK'S TIP

This dish should not be prepared too far in advance of the meal as the pears will discolour. Once peeled and cored, the pears could be kept in acidulated water *to prevent discolouring for 15-20 minutes.*

13 MELON, TOMATO AND KIWI VINAIGRETTE

Preparation time:
15 minutes

Serves 4

Calories:
273 per portion

YOU WILL NEED:
2 Ogen or Charentais melons
4 tomatoes, skinned (see Cook's Tip)
3 kiwi fruit, peeled and sliced
1 tablespoon chopped mixed herbs
   (e.g. chives, mint, parsley)
FOR THE DRESSING
4 tablespoons lemon juice
2 tablespoons clear honey
3 tablespoons olive oil
salt and pepper

First, make the dressing. Combine all the ingredients in a screw-top jar and shake well to blend.

Cut the melons in half and discard the seeds. Scoop the flesh into balls, using a melon baller, or cut into cubes; reserve the shells. Cut each tomato into 8 wedges and discard the seeds.

Place the melon in a bowl with the tomatoes, kiwi fruit and herbs. Pour over the dressing and toss well.

Spoon the mixture into the melon shells and sprinkle with pumpkin seeds, if liked.

■ COOK'S TIP

To peel tomatoes quickly and easily either put them in boiling water for 45-60 seconds, drain and peel away the skins, or spear them on a fork and turn them over a gas flame until the skin puckers and blisters, when it will be easy to peel away.

14 AVOCADO WITH CURRIED SAUCE

Preparation time:
10 minutes, plus chilling

Serves 4

Calories:
696 per portion

YOU WILL NEED:
2 ripe avocados
juice of ½ lemon
FOR THE SAUCE
1-2 teaspoons curry powder
1 garlic clove, crushed
150 ml/¼ pint mayonnaise
150 ml/¼ pint double cream
2 drops Tabasco sauce
salt and pepper
2 hard-boiled eggs, chopped
1 tablespoon chopped parsley
FOR THE GARNISH
lemon twists (see Cook's Tip)
parsley or basil leaves

First, make the sauce. Put the curry powder and garlic in a bowl and gradually mix in the mayonnaise and cream. Add the Tabasco sauce and season with salt and pepper to taste. Cover and leave in the refrigerator for 4-6 hours to allow the flavour to mellow.

Add the eggs and parsley to the sauce and stir well.

Cut the avocados in half, remove the stones and sprinkle with lemon juice.

Arrange the avocado halves on 4 individual plates. Spoon the sauce into each avocado and serve immediately, garnished with lemon twists and parsley or basil leaves.

■ COOK'S TIP

To make a lemon twist, make a cut in a lemon slice from the outer edge to the centre and twist the cut edges away from each other. Make orange twists this way.

15 AVOCADO WITH MANGO SALAD

Preparation time:
20 minutes, plus
marinating

Serves 6

Calories:
473 per portion

YOU WILL NEED:
3 ripe avocados
1 large ripe mango
little extra lemon juice
sprigs of dill or continental parsley, to garnish
FOR THE VINAIGRETTE
100 g/4 oz raspberries, fresh or frozen
150 ml/¼ pint sunflower or vegetable oil
2 tablespoons white wine vinegar
3 tablespoons lemon juice
1½ teaspoons caster sugar

Make the vinaigrette. Put the raspberries into a bowl then add the oil, vinegar and 1 tablespoon of the lemon juice and mash well together. If using frozen raspberries allow them to thaw partially before mashing. Leave to stand for 30 minutes.

Liquidize or purée the raspberry mixture then sieve to remove all the pips. Put into a clean bowl and beat in the sugar.

Just before serving, peel, quarter and slice the avocados and the mango and dip the avocado slices in the remaining lemon juice.

Spoon 2-3 tablespoons of the raspberry vinaigrette on to 6 side plates. Arrange slices of drained avocado and mango over the sauce, and garnish with a sprig of dill or continental parsley. Serve within an hour to prevent the avocados from discolouring.

16 TROUT WITH DILL

Preparation time:
5 minutes

Cooking time:
10-14 minutes

Serves 4

Calories:
283 per portion

YOU WILL NEED:
4 trout, cleaned
salt and pepper
1 tablespoon oil
4 spring onions, chopped
1 tablespoon parsley
juice of ½ lemon
few dill sprigs
FOR THE GARNISH
dill sprigs
lemon wedges

Season the trout with salt and pepper to taste. Mix together the oil, spring onions, parsley, lemon juice and dill. Divide the mixture into 4 portions and put into the cavities in the trout.

Cook under a preheated medium grill for 5-7 minutes on each side, until cooked.

Arrange on a warmed serving dish and serve immediately, garnished with dill and lemon wedges.

■ COOK'S TIP

Other suitable vegetable oils for this recipe include safflower or arachide (peanut) oil. Corn oil would be rather too heavy.

■ COOK'S TIP

Dill, sometimes called dillweed, is a plant of the parsley family and is available fresh, as used in this recipe, or dried. Dill seeds are used in pickles.

17 TROUT WITH HERBS

Preparation time:	YOU WILL NEED:
5 minutes	4 tablespoons wholewheat flour
	½ teaspoon salt
Cooking time:	¼ teaspoon pepper
12-15 minutes	4 trout, cleaned
	3 tablespoons olive oil
Serves 4	25 g/1 oz butter
	juice of ½ lemon
Calories:	1 tablespoon chopped mixed herbs
423 per portion	(parsley, chives and thyme)
	salt and pepper

Mix together the flour, salt and pepper and use to coat the trout. Heat the oil in a heavy frying pan, add the fish and fry for 5-6 minutes on each side until golden brown. Place on a warmed serving dish and keep hot.

Wipe the frying pan with kitchen paper. Add the butter and cook until golden brown. Quickly add the lemon juice, herbs, salt and pepper to taste. Pour over the trout and serve immediately.

18 PINK TROUT FILLETS IN ASPIC

Preparation time:	YOU WILL NEED:
about 40 minutes	900 ml/1½ pints water
	1 small onion
Cooking time:	few parsley stalks
about 35 minutes	pared rind of ½ lemon
	salt
Oven temperature:	½ level teaspoon black peppercorns
160 C, 325 F, gas 3	2 tablespoons lemon juice
	8 fillets pink rainbow trout
Serves 8	150 ml/¼ pint dry white wine
Calories:	1 tablespoon powdered gelatine
173 per portion	1 egg white
	2 egg shells, crushed

Put the water, onion, parsley, lemon rind, salt, peppercorns and lemon juice into a pan. Bring to the boil, cover and simmer 20 minutes. Strain into a shallow ovenproof dish, then add the fillets, skin side downwards, in a single layer. Cover and cook in a preheated oven for 5 minutes. Remove from the oven and leave undisturbed until cold.

Strain the liquor and boil until it has reduced to 350 ml/12 fl oz. Put the wine into a pan, sprinkle over the gelatine and heat gently to dissolve. Add to the fish stock with the egg white and shells. Bring to the boil, whisking. Allow the foam to rise to the top of the pan, without further stirring, then remove. Bring to the boil again, then strain through a scalded jelly bag. Cool, then chill.

Meanwhile, carefully skin each fillet and place on individual plates. Spoon or brush a thin layer of aspic over each.

▣ COOK'S TIP

Serve succulent young vegetables, such as small new potatoes, baby sweetcorn or mangetout with this dish.

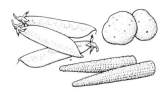

▣ COOK'S TIP

Clever garnishing adds elegance to this recipe. Dip strips of black olive and tarragon leaves in aspic then attach them in attractive patterns to the fish and its first layer of aspic. Once in place, spoon a second thin layer of aspic over the fish and its garnish. Chill until set.

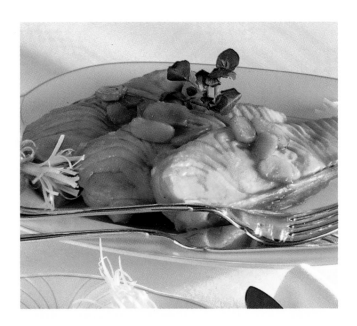

19 SWEET AND SOUR HALIBUT

Preparation time:
15 minutes, plus
marinating

Cooking time:
15 minutes

Serves 4

Calories:
248 per portion

YOU WILL NEED:
4 halibut or cod steaks, about 175-
    225 g/6-8 o ach
4 tablespoons medium sherry
1 tablespoon lemon juice
6 tablespoons orange juice
3 tablespoons soy sauce
2 tablespoons demerara sugar
salt and pepper
1 × 225 g/8 oz can water chestnuts,
    drained and sliced
FOR THE GARNISH:
spring onion tassels (see Cook's Tip)
sprigs of watercress

Lay the halibut steaks in a single layer in a dish or baking tin.
Combine the sherry, juices, soy sauce, sugar and a pinch of
salt and pepper. Pour over the fish, cover and leave in a cool
place to marinate for an hour, turning the fish over once.

Place the drained fish in a foil-lined grill pan and cook
under a moderate heat for 7-8 minutes on each side until just
cooked through. Remove the skin, if wished.

Meanwhile, transfer the marinade to a small saucepan.
Bring it to the boil and simmer for a minute or so. Add the
water chestnuts and continue to simmer gently for 3-4
minutes until the sauce begins to thicken. Taste and adjust the
seasonings.

Serve the fish with the sauce and water chestnuts spooned
over and garnished with spring onion tassels and sprigs of
watercress.

▌COOK'S TIP

To make spring onion
tassels, trim the spring
onions to about 7.5 cm/3
inches long. Cut halfway
through the stalks
lengthways 3 or 4 times.

Leave the tassels in iced
water for an hour or so to
open out.

20 MEDITERRANEAN FISH STEW

Preparation time:
25 minutes

Cooking time:
about 45 minutes

Serves 8

Calories:
252 per portion

YOU WILL NEED:
1.5 kg/3 lb assorted fish, cleaned (see
    Cook's Tip)
2 tablespoons olive oil
1 large onion, chopped
2 leeks, chopped
4 garlic cloves, crushed
450 g/1 lb tomatoes, skinned and
    chopped
1 bay leaf
1 bouquet garni
300 ml/½ pint dry white wine
few saffron strands
salt and pepper
1 loaf French bread, sliced and toasted
chopped parsley, to garnish

Remove the heads, bones and skin from the fish; put these in a
pan and cover with water. Bring to the boil and simmer for 15
minutes. Strain and reserve the stock. Cut the fish into pieces.

Heat the oil in a large pan, add the onion and leeks and
fry until golden. Add the garlic, tomatoes, herbs and wine.
Add the fish, except prawns and crab. Pour in the stock,
adding water to cover. Add saffron, salt and pepper. Bring to
the boil, cover and simmer for 10 minutes. Add the prawns
and crab; cook for 2 minutes.

Arrange the toast in the base of a large tureen, lift the fish
from the pan and pile on top. Boil the stock rapidly for 2
minutes, then strain over the fish. Sprinkle with parsley.

▌COOK'S TIP

Choose from the following
fish: cod or haddock, plaice
or sole, red or grey mullet,
bream or mackerel, scallops
or mussels, crab and prawn.

21 CHICKEN MINCEUR

Preparation time:
10 minutes

Cooking time:
2-2¼ hours

Serves 4

Calories:
316 per portion

YOU WILL NEED:
1 × 1.5 kg/3 lb roasting chicken
finely grated rind and juice of 2 limes
2 tarragon sprigs or 2 teaspoons
   tarragon in vinegar, drained
450 ml/¾ pint hot chicken stock
salt and pepper
1 Charentais melon, sliced
¼ head of curly endive
lime slices, to garnish

Use the chicken trimmings and giblets to make stock; keep on one side. Truss the chicken (see Cook's Tip).

Place the lime rind and juice, the tarragon and the stock in a flameproof casserole. Add the chicken, breast side down, cover and simmer for 1¾-2 hours, until the juices run clear, turning the chicken halfway through cooking. Cut the chicken into quarters and let cool.

Boil the cooking liquid rapidly until reduced by half; add salt and pepper to taste and leave to cool.

Arrange the melon and endive on a serving dish and lay the chicken on top. Garnish with lime slices. Spoon some of the sauce over the chicken and hand the rest separately.

22 STUFFED CHICKEN BREASTS

Preparation time:
15 minutes

Cooking time:
35-40 minutes

Oven temperature:
200 C, 400 F, gas 6

Serves 2

Calories:
275 per portion

YOU WILL NEED:
2 chicken breasts
40 g/1½ oz softened butter
50 g/2 oz ham, finely chopped
1 garlic clove, crushed
1 tablespoon grated Parmesan cheese
½ teaspoon dried or fresh rosemary,
   chopped
salt and pepper
3 tablespoons dry white wine

Wipe the chicken breasts with absorbent kitchen paper. Loosen the skin from the breasts.

Beat 25 g/1 oz of the butter with the ham, garlic, Parmesan cheese, rosemary, salt and pepper. Spread the stuffing under the skin of each chicken breast and secure with cocktail sticks.

Place the chicken in a baking dish, dot with the remaining butter, sprinkle with salt and pepper and cover with foil. Bake in a preheated oven for 30-35 minutes until tender and golden brown.

Place the chicken on a warmed serving dish and pour the cooking juices into a small saucepan. Add the wine and bring to the boil. Simmer for 2 minutes, taste and add more salt and pepper, if necessary. Pour the sauce over the chicken and serve.

■ COOK'S TIP

To truss a bird, put it back downwards, with the centre of the string beneath the tail end. Cross the string over the tail and loop each end round the opposite drumstick, pulling to bring the drumstick over the vent. Turn the bird over. Loop each end of string round an upper wing, then across the neck flap. Knot the string.

■ COOK'S TIP

If possible, buy whole Parmesan, as the cheese, when freshly grated from a large piece, has a better flavour and is less dry than ready-grated Parmesan.

23 STEWED PIGEONS IN WINE

Preparation time:
10 minutes

Cooking time:
1 hour 20 minutes

Serves 6

Calories:
995 per portion

YOU WILL NEED:
6 rashers rindless streaky bacon
3 young pigeons, cleaned
50 g/2 oz butter
2 tablespoons brandy
150 ml/¼ pint dry white wine
10 pickling onions
6 tablespoons beef stock
salt and pepper
100 g/4 oz button mushrooms
1 tablespoon chopped parsley
FOR THE GARNISH
12-16 green olives
thyme sprigs

Wrap 2 bacon rashers around each pigeon and secure with string. Melt the butter in a pan, add the pigeons and cook for 10 minutes until browned all over. Pour over the brandy and wine, bring to the boil and cook for 2 minutes. Add the onions, stock, and salt and pepper to taste. Cover and simmer for 1 hour. Add the mushrooms and parsley and cook for 5 minutes.

Transfer to a warmed serving dish and garnish with olives and thyme. Serve immediately.

24 CRISPY DUCK WITH GRAPE SAUCE

Preparation time:
5 minutes

Cooking time:
30 minutes

Oven temperature:
230 C, 450 F, gas 8

Serves 2

Calories:
822 per portion

YOU WILL NEED:
2 duck portions
1 teaspoon salt
1 teaspoon arrowroot
150 ml/¼ pint orange juice
100 g/4 oz black grapes, halved and
  seeded
FOR THE GARNISH
1 orange, sliced
2 watercress sprigs

Sprinkle the duck portions with the salt. Place on a rack in a roasting pan and cook in a preheated oven for 30 minutes.

Meanwhile, blend the arrowroot with the orange juice in a small pan. Bring to the boil, then stir in the grapes.

Transfer the duck to a warmed serving dish and pour over the sauce. Garnish with orange slices and watercress to serve.

■ COOK'S TIP

There is no close season for pigeon, but the birds are considered to be at their best between March and September, when the birds are young. A young *bird will have small pink legs, a fat breast and a flexible beak.*

■ COOK'S TIP

This recipe works well with all duck portions – breast, quarters and halves. Cooking times may be a little longer for large portions.

25 DUCK BREASTS WITH HORSERADISH SAUCE

Preparation time:
15 minutes

Cooking time:
32-35 minutes

Serves 4

Calories:
209 per portion

YOU WILL NEED:
4 duck breast portions, boned
1 tablespoon sunflower oil
FOR THE SAUCE
1 large cooking apple, peeled and
    thickly sliced
2 tablespoons water
3 tablespoons grated horseradish
65 ml/2½ fl oz soured cream
65 ml/2½ fl oz natural yogurt
1 tablespoon lemon juice

Brush the duck breasts with the oil.

Make the sauce. Put the apple with the water into a small saucepan, cover and cook for about 15 minutes until soft, stirring from time to time. Pass through a food mill into a bowl and leave to cool.

When the apple purée is tepid, stir in the horseradish, soured cream, yogurt and lemon juice.

Arrange the duck breasts skin side up on the grill rack. Place under a preheated grill and cook for 10 minutes. Turn and cook for a further 6-8 minutes. Cool.

Using a very sharp knife, cut the cooled duck breasts diagonally into thin slices. Arrange each sliced duck breast in a fan shape on a plate. Spoon a portion of horseradish sauce on to the side of each plate and serve immediately.

26 DUCK WITH PEPPERCORNS

Preparation time:
10 minutes

Cooking time:
about 1¼-1½ hours

Oven temperature:
200 C, 400 F, gas 6

Serves 6

Calories:
1,456 per portion

YOU WILL NEED:
2 × 1 kg/2 lb oven-ready ducklings
salt and pepper
25 g/1 oz butter
4 shallots, finely chopped
150 ml/¼ pint dry white wine
4 tablespoons brandy
4 tablespoons whole green
    peppercorns or 1 tablespoon black
    peppercorns, coarsely crushed
400 ml/14 fl oz double cream

Prick the skin of the ducklings with a fork and season liberally with salt and pepper. Place in a roasting pan and cook in a preheated oven for about 1¼ hours until tender.

Meanwhile, melt the butter in a pan, add the shallots and cook until transparent. Stir in the wine and brandy, bring to the boil and boil for 5 minutes.

Cut the ducklings into pieces, arrange on a warmed serving dish and keep hot. Add the peppercorns and cream to the sauce and season with salt to taste. Cook for 3-5 minutes until thickened.

Spoon the sauce over the ducklings and serve immediately.

■ COOK'S TIP

An elegant green salad would go well with this cold duck recipe. Try combining less usual ingredients such as batavia, radicchio, sorrel, lamb's lettuce and thinly sliced mushrooms, with a light oil and wine vinegar and lemon juice dressing.

■ COOK'S TIP

This recipe works well with duckling or duck portions. Cooking time will be less – 30-40 minutes, depending on the size of the portions.

27 LAMB STUFFED WITH PINE NUTS AND CORIANDER

Preparation time:
10 minutes

Cooking time:
2⅓-3 hours

Oven temperature:
180 C, 350 F, gas 4

Serves 4

Calories:
559 per portion

YOU WILL NEED:
2 kg/4½ lb leg of lamb, boned and
    trimmed of fat (see Cook's Tip)
3 tablespoons olive oil
1 tablespoon coriander seeds, crushed
4 garlic cloves, peeled and crushed
salt and pepper
FOR THE STUFFING
65 g/2½ oz long-grain rice, cooked
    and drained
50 g/2 oz currants or seedless raisins
50 g/2 oz pine nuts
½ teaspoon ground cinnamon
salt and pepper
½ egg, beaten

Pat the lamb dry with absorbent kitchen paper. Combine the oil with the coriander seeds, garlic and salt and pepper to taste and rub the lamb inside and out with the mixture.

In a bowl combine all the stuffing ingredients and stir well to mix. Spoon into the cavity in the lamb. Roll the lamb and tie in several places with fine string, or secure with meat skewers.

Place the stuffed lamb in a large roasting tin and roast in a preheated oven for 2½-3 hours, until done to your liking, basting from time to time.

Transfer the lamb to a warmed carving dish and serve carved into slices.

28 LAMB CUTLETS WITH SHERRY SAUCE

Preparation time:
20 minutes, plus
chilling

Cooking time:
15-20 minutes

Serves 4

Calories:
728 per portion

YOU WILL NEED:
8 lamb cutlets
1 garlic clove, sliced
1 egg, beaten
50 g/2 oz white breadcrumbs
1-2 tablespoons oil
25 g/1 oz unsalted butter
1 tablespoon each chopped thyme,
    parsley, sage and chives
150 ml/¼ pint dry sherry
150 ml/¼ pint double cream
salt and pepper
FOR THE GARNISH
100 g/4 oz green olives
sage leaves

Cut small slits in the cutlets and push in the slivered garlic. Coat each cutlet with egg and breadcrumbs, then chill for 20 minutes.

Heat the oil and butter in a frying pan, add the cutlets and brown on both sides. Lower the heat and cook for 6 minutes on each side. Drain on absorbent kitchen paper and arrange on a warmed serving dish; keep warm.

Add the herbs and sherry to the pan and boil rapidly for 2 minutes, until thickened. Stir in the cream, and salt and pepper to taste.

Spoon over the cutlets and serve immediately, garnished with the olives and sage.

■ COOK'S TIP

Although a leg of lamb is not too difficult to bone, the butcher will make a neater job of it: give him some warning of your requirements.

■ COOK'S TIP

Lamb cutlets are taken from the best end of neck. They are the neatest of the various lamb chops available and so are ideal for this recipe. They cook *more quickly than leg, chump or loin chops, and the meat is very tender.*

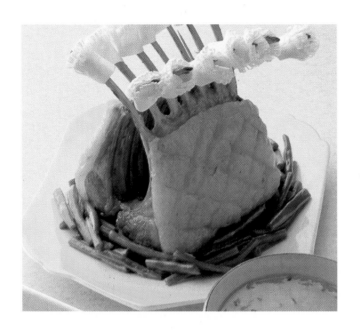

29 GUARD OF HONOUR

Preparation time:
15 minutes

Cooking time:
1¼ hours

Oven temperature:
180 C, 350 F, gas 4

Serves 6

Calories:
541 per portion

YOU WILL NEED:
2 best end necks of lamb
FOR THE SAUCE
25 g/1 oz butter
2 rashers rindless streaky bacon,
  chopped
1 small onion
50 g/2 oz mushrooms
1 small carrot
25 g/1 oz flour
300 ml/½ pint beef stock
1 teaspoon dried mixed herbs (see
  Cook's Tip)
2 tablespoons tomato purée
salt and pepper
2 tablespoons sherry
2 tablespoons redcurrant jelly
2 tablespoons green peppercorns

For the sauce, melt the butter in a pan, add the bacon and fry for 2 minutes. Chop the vegetables, add to the pan and fry for 5 minutes. Stir in the flour, then gradually stir in the stock. Bring to the boil. Add the herbs, tomato purée, and salt and pepper. Cover and simmer for 1 hour. Sieve the sauce into a clean pan and add the remaining ingredients.

Scrape clean the tips of the lamb bones. Sew the cutlets together to form an arch shape and cover the tips with foil. Roast in a preheated oven for about 1 hour, until tender.

Replace the foil with cutlet frills, transfer the lamb to a warmed serving dish and serve with the warmed sauce.

■ COOK'S TIP

Mixed herbs may be bought ready-prepared in packs. The usual mixture is thyme, marjoram, parsley, rosemary and basil, a good mixture for lamb.

30 TOURNEDOS EN CROÛTE

Preparation time:
20 minutes, plus
cooling

Cooking time:
20-25 minutes

Oven temperature:
200 C, 400 F, gas 6

Serves 4

Calories:
638 per portion

YOU WILL NEED:
butter for frying
4 fillet steaks (tournedos)
salt and pepper
100 g/4 oz liver pâté
2 tablespoons brandy or dry sherry
225 g/8 oz puff pastry
1 egg, beaten, to glaze

Melt a knob of butter in a large frying pan and heat until foaming. Add the steaks to the pan and sauté for about 1 minute on each side. Remove from the pan, season to taste and set aside to cool.

Soften the liver pâté with the brandy or sherry and spread over the steaks.

Roll out the pastry into four squares large enough to encase the steaks. Wrap the squares around the steaks, sealing the edges with a little water. Use the pastry trimmings to decorate the tops of the parcels with leaves, flowers, etc. Brush with beaten egg.

Place on a baking sheet and put into a preheated oven. Bake for 15-20 minutes or until the pastry is golden. Serve the tournedos immediately.

■ COOK'S TIP

These elegant steaks require unfussy accompaniments: choose a crisp green salad or a vegetable dish such as ratatouille (see recipe 60).

31 STEAKS WITH STILTON

Preparation time:
10 minutes, plus
chilling

Cooking time:
6-10 minutes

Serves 6

Calories:
416 per portion

YOU WILL NEED:
75 g/3 oz blue Stilton cheese
75 g/3 oz butter, softened
1 tablespoon port
1 teaspoon each chopped chives and
  thyme
½ garlic clove, crushed
salt and pepper
6 × 2.5cm/1 inch thick fillet steaks
thyme sprigs, to garnish

Put the cheese, butter and port in a blender or food processor and blend until smooth. Stir in the herbs, garlic and salt and pepper to taste. Form the mixture into a roll, wrap in foil and chill in the freezer for 20 minutes.

Season the steaks with salt and pepper and cook under a preheated hot grill for 3-5 minutes on each side, according to taste. Arrange on a warmed serving dish.

Cut the butter into 6 and place on the steaks. Garnish with thyme and serve immediately.

32 BLANQUETTE DE VEAU

Preparation time:
20 minutes

Cooking time:
2 hours

Serves 6

Calories:
205 per portion

YOU WILL NEED:
1 kg/2 lb pie veal, cubed
2 onions, chopped
2 carrots, sliced
1 tablespoon lemon juice
2 bay leaves
salt and pepper
50 g/2 oz butter
50 g/2 oz plain flour
3 tablespoons single cream
FOR THE GARNISH
6 rashers rindless streaky bacon
1 lemon, cut into wedges
parsley sprigs

Put the veal in a pan with the vegetables, lemon juice, bay leaves and salt and pepper. Add water to cover and simmer, covered, for 1½ hours. Remove the meat and vegetables from the pan with a slotted spoon. Discard the bay leaf. Strain the stock, reserving about 600 ml/1 pint.

Melt the butter in the pan and stir in the flour. Gradually add the reserved stock and bring to the boil. Remove from the heat and stir in the cream. Check the seasoning and return the meat and vegetables to the pan. Heat through very gently. Meanwhile, roll up the bacon rashers tightly and thread on to a skewer. Place under a preheated hot grill and cook, turning occasionally until crisp.

Transfer the veal to a dish and garnish with the bacon rolls, lemon and parsley.

■ COOK'S TIP

Serve this rich-tasting main
course with light green
vegetables, such as
courgettes, or a green salad.

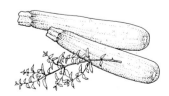

■ COOK'S TIP

This delicately-flavoured
dish requires
accompaniments that will
enhance and not overwhelm
it. Rice or noodles are usual
accompaniments, and

vegetables such as
mangetout or baby corn
would also be good.

33 ITALIAN VEAL ROLLS

Preparation time:
15 minutes

Cooking time:
30-40 minutes

Serves 6

Calories:
302 per portion

YOU WILL NEED:
6 thin slices ham
6 veal escalopes, each weighing
*   50 g/2 oz, beaten flat*
50 g/2 oz pork fat, finely chopped
1 garlic clove, sliced
2 tablespoons pine nuts
2 tablespoons sultanas
2 tablespoons grated Parmesan cheese
3 tablespoons chopped parsley
6 slices Gruyère cheese
salt and pepper
1 tablespoon oil
300 ml/½ pint dry white wine
1 tablespoon tomato purée

Lay a slice of ham on each escalope. Sprinkle with the pork fat, garlic, pine nuts, sultanas, Parmesan cheese and 1 tablespoon of the parsley. Top with Gruyère cheese and season well with salt and pepper. Roll up and secure with cocktail sticks.

Heat the oil in a pan, add the veal rolls and brown on all sides. Pour over the wine, season well and bring to the boil. Cover and simmer for 25-30 minutes, until tender. Remove the rolls from the pan with a slotted spoon and arrange on a warmed serving dish. Keep warm.

Boil the liquid in the pan until reduced by half, then stir in the tomato purée and remaining parsley. Spoon the sauce over the veal rolls.

34 SKEWERED SICILIAN PORK

Preparation time:
15 minutes, plus
marinating

Cooking time:
20 minutes

Serves 4

Calories:
479 per portion

YOU WILL NEED:
750 g/1½ lb pork fillet
4 × 2.5 cm/1 inch slices French bread,
*   quartered*
8 small slices Parma ham or streaky
*   bacon rashers, halved and rolled up*
sage and bay leaves
FOR THE MARINADE
4 tablespoons olive oil
2 tablespoons lemon juice
1 garlic clove, crushed
1 tablespoon mixed herbs
salt and pepper

Cut the pork into 2.5 cm/1 inch cubes. Put the marinade ingredients in a bowl, with salt and pepper to taste, and mix well. Add the pork cubes and marinate for 1-2 hours, turning occasionally. Remove the meat from the marinade with a slotted spoon; reserve the marinade.

Arrange the pork, French bread and Parma ham or bacon rolls alternately on 8 skewers, interspersing with sage and bay leaves to taste.

Cook under a preheated moderate grill for 10 minutes on each side, until the pork is tender and browned, basting with the remaining marinade during cooking.

Serve hot, with vegetables.

■ COOK'S TIP

Plainly cooked rice and a green salad make ideal acompaniments for this typically Italian dish.

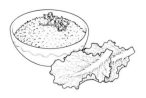

■ COOK'S TIP

These skewers of pork will cook well over a charcoal grill for a barbecue.

35 TONGUE WITH SHERRY SAUCE

Preparation time:
20 minutes, plus soaking

Cooking time:
2¾-3¼ hours

Serves 8

Calories:
667 per portion

YOU WILL NEED:
1 cured ox tongue, about 1.5 kg/3½ lb
1 onion
2 bay leaves
pepper
FOR THE SAUCE
40 g/1½ oz butter
40 g/1½ oz plain flour
150 ml/¼ pint sweet sherry
2 tablespoons redcurrant jelly
watercress sprigs, to garnish

Soak the tongue overnight in cold water. Drain and put in a large pan, cover with cold water and bring to the boil. Boil for 5 minutes then drain again. Add fresh cold water to cover the tongue, the onion, bay leaves and pepper to taste. Bring to the boil and simmer for 2½-3 hours, skimming frequently.

Drain, reserving 150 ml/¼ pint of the cooking liquid, and plunge into cold water. Remove the skin and bones. Slice the tongue thickly, arrange on a warmed serving dish and keep warm.

For the sauce, melt the butter in a pan and stir in the flour. Gradually stir in the sherry and reserved cooking liquid. Bring to the boil and simmer for 5 minutes. Add the redcurrant jelly and check the seasoning.

Pour the sauce over the tongue and serve garnished with watercress.

36 MELITZANO SALATA

Preparation time:
10 minutes, plus chilling

Cooking time:
20 minutes

Serves 6

Calories:
94 per portion

YOU WILL NEED:
2 large aubergines, about 450 g/1 lb
    total weight
1 small onion, roughly chopped
2 garlic cloves, roughly chopped
4 tablespoons olive oil
2 tablespoons lemon juice
salt and pepper
FOR THE GARNISH
parsley sprigs
lime slices

Thread the aubergines on to a skewer. Place them on the greased grill of a preheated barbecue and cook for 10 minutes, then turn the aubergines over and cook for a further 10 minutes.

Leave the aubergines until they are sufficiently cool to handle, then peel them and chop the flesh on a wooden board.

Put the aubergine flesh into a liquidizer or food processor with the onion, garlic, olive oil, lemon juice and salt and pepper to taste; blend until smooth. Cover and chill.

Transfer the purée to a bowl and garnish with the sprigs of parsley and slices of lime. Serve with pitta bread.

■ COOK'S TIP

When buying tongue, look for one with as smooth a skin as possible: a rough tongue indicates an older, and therefore tougher, one.

■ COOK'S TIP

This Greek dip has a much better flavour if the aubergines are scorched over the barbecue; if barbecuing is impossible they may be baked in a preheated oven (180C, 350F, gas 4) for 45-50 minutes.

37 GUACAMOLE

Preparation time:
10 minutes, plus
chilling time

Serves 4-6

Calories:
47-32 per portion

YOU WILL NEED:
2 ripe avocados
1 garlic clove, crushed
½ onion, chopped
1 tablespoon lime juice
2 drops Tabasco sauce
4 tomatoes, skinned, seeded and
    chopped (see recipe 13)
2 tablespoons chopped parsley
salt and pepper
1 teaspoon chilli powder
lime slices, to garnish

Peel, halve and stone the avocados. Purée the avocado flesh in an electric blender, with the garlic, onion, lime juice, Tabasco, tomatoes and parsley, until smooth. Season liberally with salt and pepper, add the chilli powder and blend again until thoroughly mixed.

Pile into a serving dish and chill for 1 hour. Garnish with lime slices and serve with Melba toast (see recipe 63).

38 MIXED VEGETABLE SALAD

Preparation time:
15 minutes, plus
chilling

Cooking time:
20-25 minutes

Serves 4

Calories:
112 per portion

YOU WILL NEED:
2 tablespoons olive oil
1-2 garlic cloves, crushed
8 button onions
2 courgettes, sliced
100 g/4 oz mushrooms
few cauliflower florets
2 celery sticks, chopped
1 × 397 g/14 oz can tomatoes
6 coriander seeds
1 bouquet garni
4 tablespoons dry white wine
1 tablespoon green peppercorns
    (optional)
salt
coriander or parsley sprigs, to garnish

Heat the oil in a pan, add the garlic and cook for 2 minutes, without browning. Stir in the onions, courgettes, mushrooms, cauliflower and celery.

Add the tomatoes with their juice and bring to the boil. Add the coriander seeds, bouquet garni, wine, peppercorns if using, and salt to taste. Simmer rapidly for 15-20 minutes, until the vegetables are just tender and the liquid reduced. Discard the bouquet garni and leave to cool.

Spoon into a serving dish and chill until required. Garnish with coriander or parsley before serving.

■ COOK'S TIP

Cover the Guacamole tightly with cling film to prevent it discolouring in the refrigerator, and do not chill it for more than 1 hour, as longer in the refrigerator may also cause it to lose its pretty green colour.

■ COOK'S TIP

If the green peppercorns are omitted, give this dish added bite with freshly ground black pepper to taste.

39 MARINATED MUSHROOMS

Preparation time:
10 minutes

Cooking time:
12 minutes

Serves 6

Calories:
120 per portion

YOU WILL NEED:
4 tablespoons oil
2 garlic cloves, crushed
1 small onion, finely chopped
2 bay leaves
1 thyme sprig
1 rosemary sprig
2 parsley sprigs
100 ml/⅓ pint dry white wine
4-6 peppercorns
12 coriander seeds
750 g/1½ lb button mushrooms
salt
chopped parsley, to garnish

Heat the oil in a pan, add the garlic and onion and cook for 10 minutes, without browning. Stir in the herbs and wine, bring to the boil and simmer for 2 minutes. Add the peppercorns, coriander seeds, mushrooms and salt to taste. Toss the mushrooms in the wine sauce until well coated.

Transfer to a bowl, cover and chill for 3-4 hours, stirring occasionally. Spoon into a serving dish and sprinkle over the parsley.

■ COOK'S TIP

These mushrooms make a good first course, served with French bread, wholemeal rolls or granary rolls.

40 GREEN FRUIT SALAD

Preparation time:
about 40 minutes, plus chilling

Cooking time:
about 9 minutes

Serves 8

Calories:
230 per portion

YOU WILL NEED:
2 limes
300 ml/½ pint water
175 g/6 oz caster sugar
150 ml/¼ pint white wine
1 small green-fleshed melon
225 g/8 oz seedless green grapes
1 firm pear
2 grapefruit
3 kiwi fruit
1 ripe avocado
2 green-skinned dessert apples

Pare the rind thinly from the limes, and cut it into julienne strips. Put into a saucepan with the water, bring to the boil and simmer for 5 minutes. Strain the lime rind; reserve the cooking liquor and make it up to 300 ml/½ pint. Add the sugar, heat slowly until it has dissolved, then boil for 2-3 minutes. Add the wine and pour the syrup into a glass bowl.

Halve and seed the melon. Scoop out the flesh with a melon baller. Add the melon balls to the syrup in the bowl. Wash the grapes and add them to the syrup. Peel, core and slice the pear; cut away the peel and pith from the grapefruit and ease out the segments from between the membranes. Add both to the syrup. Peel and slice the kiwi fruit and add to the salad. Cover, then chill for 2-3 hours.

Squeeze the juice from the limes. Peel and dice the avocado, toss it in the lime juice, drain and add to the salad. Core and slice the apples, toss in the lime juice and add to the salad, with the lime juice. Sprinkle over the reserved strips of peel.

■ COOK'S TIP

With this salad serve light sweet biscuits such as the Hazelnut and orange tuiles (recipe 51) or langues de chats.

41 MONTE BIANCO

Preparation time:
15 minutes, plus
chilling

Serves 2

Calories:
424 per portion

YOU WILL NEED:
175 g/6 oz canned chestnut purée
2 tablespoons dark rum
25 g/1 oz icing sugar
FOR THE TOPPING
4 tablespoons double or whipping
* cream*
1 teaspoon caster sugar
1 teaspoon dark rum
little plain chocolate, grated

Beat the chestnut purée until smooth. Mix in the rum and icing sugar. Divide between two glasses.

Make the topping. Whip the cream until it just holds its shape. Fold in the sugar and rum. Swirl on to the chestnut purée and chill until ready to serve.

Outline the swirl of cream with grated chocolate.

42 ORANGE SORBET

Preparation time:
20 minutes, plus
freezing

Cooking time:
20 minutes

Serves 6

Calories:
194 per portion

YOU WILL NEED:
175 g/6 oz caster sugar
450 ml/¾ pint water
6 large oranges
1 tablespoon lemon juice
3 egg whites, whisked
shredded orange rind, to decorate

Place the sugar and water in a pan and heat gently, stirring until dissolved. Bring to the boil, simmer for 15 minutes, then leave to cool.

Cut off the tops of the oranges. Using a sharp knife, remove as much flesh from the insides as possible. Reserve the orange shells.

Add the flesh to the syrup with the lemon juice, then sieve into a rigid freezerproof container. Cover, seal and freeze for about 2 hours, until mushy.

Whisk the egg whites into the orange mixture. Spoon into the orange shells and place in a freezer-proof container; freeze until firm.

Transfer to the refrigerator 1 hour before serving to soften. Decorate with shredded orange rind to serve.

■ COOK'S TIP

Use any leftover chestnut purée in stuffing, or mixed with whipped cream to sandwich between meringues. It may also be frozen for use later.

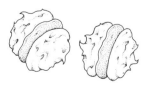

■ COOK'S TIP

This sorbet may be frozen in the freezerproof container without using the orange skins, allowing it to be served in scoops, perhaps with other-flavour sorbets.

43 CHOCOLATE MINT ICE

Preparation time:
20 minutes, plus
freezing

Serves 8

Calories:
182 per portion

YOU WILL NEED:
2 egg whites
100 g/4 oz caster sugar
*1 × 410 g/14½ oz can evaporated
milk, chilled*
4 drops of green food colouring
½ teaspoon peppermint essence
*75 g/3 oz plain chocolate, finely
chopped*

Whisk the egg whites until stiff, then gradually whisk in the
sugar. Place the evaporated milk in a bowl with the colouring
and peppermint essence. Whisk until thick, then fold into the
meringue mixture with the chocolate.

Turn into a rigid freezerproof container, cover, seal and
freeze for 2 hours.

Remove from the freezer and stir vigorously. Re-freeze
until firm.

Transfer to the refrigerator 1 hour before serving to
soften. Scoop into chilled glass dishes to serve.

44 ICED CHOCOLATE SOUFFLES

Preparation time:
25 minutes, plus
cooling

Cooking time:
about 5 minutes

Serves 6

Calories:
392 per portion

YOU WILL NEED:
4 eggs, separated
100 g/4 oz icing sugar, sifted
75 g/3 oz plain chocolate, chopped
1 tablespoon water
250 ml/8 fl oz double cream
2 tablespoons rum
grated chocolate, to decorate

Tie a double band of foil very tightly around 6 freezerproof
ramekin dishes to stand 2.5 cm/1 inch above the rim.

Place the egg yolks and icing sugar in a bowl and whisk
with an electric mixer until thick and creamy.

Place the chocolate and water in a small pan and heat
very gently until melted. Cool slightly, then whisk into the egg
mixture.

Whip the cream with the rum until it stands in soft peaks,
then fold into the chocolate mixture.

Whisk the egg whites until stiff and carefully fold into the
mousse. Pour into the prepared ramekins and freeze for 4
hours until firm.

To serve, remove the foil carefully. Sprinkle the grated
chocolate over the top to cover completely.

■ COOK'S TIP

*Serve this mint ice with
wafers or dessert biscuits
such as the Hazelnut and
orange tuiles (recipe 51) or
the Almond curls (recipe
223).*

■ COOK'S TIP

*These soufflés should be
transferred from the freezer
to the refrigerator about 10
minutes before serving, to
allow them to soften.*

45 ROSE PETAL TART

Preparation time:
15 minutes, plus
cooling

Cooking time:
20-25 minutes

Oven temperature:
200 C, 400 F, gas 6

Serves 6

Calories:
357 per portion

YOU WILL NEED:

225 g/8 oz flaky or puff pastry,
*   thawed if frozen*
150 ml/¼ pint natural yogurt
1 egg yolk
2 tablespoons caster sugar
300 ml/½ pint double or whipping
*   cream, whipped*
2 tablespoons rosewater
frosted petals (see Cook's Tip)

Roll out the pastry to about 5 mm/¼ inch thickness and cut out a 25 cm/10 inch circle. Place on a lightly moistened baking sheet and bake for about 20-25 minutes until the pastry is well risen, brown and dry underneath. Leave for at least 1 hour to cool completely.

Fold the yogurt, egg yolk and sugar into the whipped cream. Whisk in the rosewater.

Spoon the rosewater cream over the pastry base. Decorate with frosted rose petals and serve immediately.

46 CLEMENTINES IN ORANGE LIQUEUR

Preparation time:
10 minutes, plus
cooling time

Cooking time:
20-25 minutes

Serves 4

Calories:
241 per portion

YOU WILL NEED:

175 g/6 oz caster sugar
600 ml/1 pint water
8 clementines, peeled, reserving a little
*   rind for decoration, and pith*
*   removed*
2 tablespoons orange liqueur (see
*   Cook's Tip)*
mint sprig, to decorate

Put the sugar and water into a pan and bring to the boil, stirring constantly until the sugar has dissolved. Add the fruit, bring to the boil, then simmer for 10 minutes. Leave to cool.

Remove the fruit, boil down the syrup until reduced to about 300 ml/½ pint. Cool, then add the liqueur. Pour over the clementines and decorate with the mint sprig.

■ COOK'S TIP

To make frosted rose petals, gently wipe clean fresh, unbruised petals and, using a small, soft brush, brush them with egg white which has been whisked to form stiff peaks. Then sprinkle a little caster sugar over the petals and leave to dry.

■ COOK'S TIP

Orange liqueurs suitable for this recipe are Grand Marnier (cognac brandy with orange) and Cointreau, a colourless distillation of orange and alcohol.

47 MELON AND RASPBERRIES IN SAUTERNES

Preparation time:
5 minutes, plus chilling

Serves 4

Calories:
90 per portion

YOU WILL NEED:
1 small ripe Galia melon
175 g/6 oz fresh raspberries
½ bottle Sauternes, chilled

Halve the melon and either scoop out small balls using a melon baller or cut the flesh into small cubes.

Divide the melon and raspberries equally between 4 glass dishes. Pour over any melon juice, cover and chill in the refrigerator for at least 2 hours.

Just before serving, pour the chilled Sauternes into each dish to almost cover the melon and raspberries. Serve immediately.

48 CARAMELIZED PINEAPPLE

Preparation time:
20 minutes, plus standing

Cooking time:
20 minutes

Serves 4

Calories:
322 per portion

YOU WILL NEED:
1 medium pineapple
1 cinnamon stick
300 ml/½ pint water
225 g/8 oz white sugar
150 ml/¼ pint unsweetened orange juice
2 tablespoons white rum (optional)

Cut the pineapple into 1-2 cm/½-¾ inch slices and remove the skin. Cut each slice into quarters or sixths and place in a serving bowl.

Break the cinnamon stick into 2 or 3 pieces, and put into a heavy-based saucepan with the water and sugar. Heat gently until the sugar has dissolved, stirring occasionally, then bring to the boil.

Boil hard, uncovered, and without further stirring until the mixture becomes a caramel colour. Remove immediately from the heat and carefully pour in the orange juice.

When all the caramel has dissolved (heating it again gently, if necessary) pour it over the pineapple, adding the rum, if using. Cover and leave to stand in a cool place for at least 6 hours, and up to 24 hours before serving. It is a good idea to give it a stir occasionally so all the pineapple is evenly coated in the syrup. Before serving, remove the pieces of cinnamon stick.

■ COOK'S TIP

Frozen raspberries may be used instead of fresh ones, though they will not be quite so firm. They should be thoroughly thawed before being used.

■ COOK'S TIP

Cinnamon is an aromatic bark. Do not use ground cinnamon in this recipe, as it does not dissolve and will speckle the syrup.

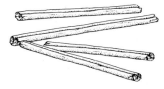

49 PETITS VACHERINS AUX NOIX

Preparation time:
20 minutes

Cooking time:
1½-2 hours

Oven temperature:
130 C, 250 F, gas ½

Serves 6

Calories:
263 per portion

YOU WILL NEED:
FOR THE MERINGUE
2 egg whites
100 g/4 oz soft brown sugar
50 g/2 oz walnuts, ground
FOR THE FILLING
2 tablespoons rum
150 ml/¼ pint double cream
6 walnut halves, to decorate

Whisk the egg whites until stiff, then whisk in the sugar, a tablespoon at a time. Carefully fold in the walnuts.

Line two baking sheets with silicone paper and draw six 7.5 cm/3 inch circles and six 5 cm/2 inch circles. Put the meringue into a piping bag fitted with a 1 cm/1 inch plain nozzle and pipe on to the circles to cover completely.

Bake in a preheated oven for 1½-2 hours. Transfer to a wire rack to cool.

Place the rum and cream in a bowl and whip until stiff. Put into a piping bag fitted with a large fluted nozzle and pipe three-quarters on to the large circles. Cover with the smaller circles. Decorate with the remaining cream and the walnut halves.

50 PRALINE CHARLOTTE

Preparation time:
20 minutes, plus
cooling and chilling

Cooking time:
10-12 minutes

Serves 6

Calories:
410 per portion

YOU WILL NEED:
1 ×recipe praline (see Cook's Tip)
18 sponge fingers
3 egg yolks
3 tablespoons icing sugar, sifted
350 ml/12 fl oz milk
15g/½ oz gelatine, soaked in 3 tablespoons cold water
300 ml/½ pint whipping cream, whipped
4 tablespoons double cream, whipped, to decorate

Make the praline. Trim one end off each sponge finger to a height of a 1.5 litre/2½ pint charlotte mould. Fit them closely, rounded end down, around the side of the lightly oiled mould.

Beat the egg yolks and icing sugar together until creamy. Bring the milk to the boil, then stir in the egg mixture. Return to the pan and cook gently, stirring until thickened. Strain into a bowl, add the gelatine and stir until dissolved. Cool.

Add three-quarters of the praline and stir over a bowl of iced water until the mixture starts to thicken. Fold in the 300 ml/½ pint cream, pour into the prepared mould and chill until set.

To serve, invert on to a plate and decorate with the 4 tablespoons cream and remaining praline.

■ COOK'S TIP

Put the meringues together as near to serving time as possible. Whip the rum and cream stiffly, put into a piping bag and keep in the refrigerator is needed.

■ COOK'S TIP

To make praline heat 50 g/2 oz whole almonds and 50 g/2 oz caster sugar gently until the sugar has melted, then cook until nut brown. Turn out on to

an oiled baking sheet. When the praline is hard crush it with a rolling pin.

51 HAZELNUT AND ORANGE TUILES

Preparation time:
10 minutes

Cooking time:
about 30 minutes

Oven temperature:
190 C, 375 F, gas 5

Makes about 20

Calories:
36 per biscuit

YOU WILL NEED:
1 egg white
50 g/2 oz caster sugar
25 g/1 oz plain flour, sifted
25 g/1 oz toasted hazelnuts, finely chopped
finely grated rind of ½ orange
25 g/1 oz butter, melted

Line 2 baking sheets with non-stick silicone paper. Lightly grease a rolling pin and stand it on a wire rack.

Whisk the egg white until very stiff and fold in the sugar, flour and hazelnuts and then the orange rind. Mix gently but thoroughly. Fold in the cooled but still runny butter.

Put teaspoons of the mixture on to the baking sheets, keeping them well apart and spread out thinly; 4 or 5 per sheet is ample. Cook in a preheated oven for about 8 minutes or until browned around the edges and a very pale brown in the centre.

Cool only very briefly and then remove from the paper, using a palette knife, and lay over the rolling pin so they form a curl as they cool and set. When cold and firm, remove and store in an airtight container.

Use the rest of the mixture to make more tuiles.

52 ALMOND PETITS FOURS

Preparation time:
15 minutes

Cooking time:
20-25 minutes

Oven temperature:
150 C, 300 F, gas 2

Makes about 24

Calories:
42 per petit four

YOU WILL NEED:
100 g/4 oz ground almonds
100 g/4 oz caster sugar
few drops almond essence
2 egg whites, whisked until stiff
flaked almonds or glacé cherries, to decorate

Stir the ground almonds, caster sugar and almond essence into the egg whites.

Line a baking sheet with non-stick silicone or greased greaseproof paper. Place the mixture in a piping bag with a large star nozzle and pipe the mixture into circles, S-shapes and sticks. Put a flaked almond or piece of glacé cherry on to each of the petits fours.

Bake in a preheated oven for 20-25 minutes. Cool on a wire tray.

■ COOK'S TIP

These biscuits are good served with desserts like sorbet or fruit salad, providing a delicious contrast in textures.

■ COOK'S TIP

Serve these light and pretty biscuits as a delicious contrast to the taste of after-dinner coffee.

SUPPER PARTIES

This is the chapter in which to find those quick and easy-to-prepare dishes ideal for serving to friends informally, perhaps after the theatre or a concert, or while watching something special on TV. And there are recipes which can be prepared ahead for easy serving later.

53 ICED TOMATO AND BASIL SOUP

Preparation time:
15 minutes

Cooking time:
about 1 hour

Serves 6

Calories:
108 per portion

YOU WILL NEED:
1 tablespoon oil
1 large onion, chopped
1 garlic clove, crushed
25 g/1 oz flour
1 kg/2 lb ripe tomatoes, chopped
1 tablespoon Worcestershire sauce
2 drops Tabasco sauce
250 ml/8 fl oz dry white wine
1 tablespoon tomato purée
salt and pepper
3 tablespoons chopped basil
FOR THE GARNISH
6 tablespoons double cream, whipped
chopped chives

Heat the oil in a large pan, add the onion and garlic and cook for 5 minutes without browning. Stir in the flour and cook, stirring, for 2 minutes. Add the tomatoes, cover and cook gently for 20 minutes, stirring occasionally. Add the Worcestershire and Tabasco sauces, wine, tomato purée, and salt and pepper to taste. Bring to the boil, cover and simmer for 30 minutes. Cool slightly.

Sieve or work in an electric blender until smooth then strain into a bowl. Leave to cool, then stir in the basil and chill for several hours.

Pour into individual soup bowls. Top each with a swirl of cream and chopped chives. Serve immediately.

54 FRENCH ONION SOUP

Preparation time:
15 minutes

Cooking time:
50 minutes – 1 hour

Serves 4

Calories:
324 per portion

YOU WILL NEED:
50 g/2 oz butter
750 g/1½ lb onions, thinly sliced
2 teaspoons sugar
2 teaspoons plain flour
1 litre/1¾ pints beef stock
salt and pepper
½ French loaf, sliced
50 g/2 oz Gruyère cheese, grated

Melt the butter in a pan, add the onions and sugar. Lower the heat and cook the onions slowly for 20-30 minutes, until they are an even chestnut brown. Take care to cook them slowly, so that they brown evenly and to a good colour but without burning.

Add the flour and cook for about 5 minutes, stirring well. Add the stock, salt and pepper. Bring to the boil and simmer for 15-20 minutes.

Meanwhile, place the slices of French bread under a pre-heated grill and toast on one side. Cover the other side with the grated cheese and toast until golden brown.

Taste and adjust the seasoning, then pour the soup into a hot tureen. Place a piece of toast in each serving dish and pour the soup over.

■ COOK'S TIP

If calorie-counting is a consideration, replace the double cream in the garnish with a spoonful of natural yogurt.

■ COOK'S TIP

Although the cheese toast should be made just before serving, the soup itself may be made well in advance of the meal and reheated gently but thoroughly.

55 FENNEL SOUP WITH GARLIC CROUTONS

Preparation time:
30 minutes

Cooking time:
40 minutes

Serves 2

Calories:
255 per portion

YOU WILL NEED:
1 small bulb fennel, weighing about
    200 g/7 oz
1 small onion, chopped
300 ml/½ pint chicken stock
salt and pepper
150 ml/¼ pint milk
1 teaspoon lemon juice
3 tablespoons natural yogurt or single
    or soured cream
1 egg yolk
garlic croûtons (see recipe 6)

Cut any sprigs of green from the fennel and reserve for garnish; chop the remainder of the bulb. Place in a saucepan with the onion, stock and seasonings. Bring to the boil, cover the pan and simmer gently for 30 minutes until tender.

Leave to cool a little, then purée, liquidize or sieve the soup and return to a clean pan. Add the milk and lemon juice and bring to the boil. Blend the yogurt with the egg yolk, add a little of the soup then whisk back into the pan of soup. Heat gently without boiling. Meanwhile, make the croûtons (see Cook's Tip).

To serve, taste and adjust the seasoning of the soup and reheat without boiling. Garnish with the reserved sprigs of fennel and serve with the garlic croûtons.

56 CHICK PEA SOUP

Preparation time:
20 minutes, plus
soaking

Cooking time:
about 1¼ hours

Serves 6

Calories:
125 per portion

YOU WILL NEED:
100 g/4 oz chick peas, soaked
    overnight (see Cook's Tip)
2 onions, chopped
2 rashers lean bacon, chopped
1-2 garlic cloves, crushed
2 tablespoons oil
2 tablespoons tomato purée
1 tablespoon plain flour
1 x 425 g/15 oz can tomatoes, puréed
1 litre/1¾ pint stock or water
salt and pepper
1 teaspoon light soft brown sugar
2 bay leaves
50 g/2 oz noodles
fat or oil, for frying

Drain the chick peas. Put the onions and bacon into a pan with the garlic and oil and cook gently, stirring for 5 minutes. Add the tomato purée and flour and cook for a minute or so. Gradually add the puréed tomatoes, then the stock, stirring all the time, and bring to the boil. Season, then add the brown sugar, bay leaves and chick peas. Cover the pan. Simmer for about 50 minutes, until the chick peas are very tender.

Break the noodles into lengths, about 2.5 cm/1 inch long, and cook in boiling salted water for 6 minutes. Drain well and dry on kitchen paper. Heat the oil to about 150 C/325 F and fry the noodles a few at a time, for about 1 minute until they are very pale brown and crispy. Drain. Pour the soup into a tureen and serve sprinkled with the fried noodles.

■ COOK'S TIP

For this amount of soup, make the garlic croûtons from three slices of white bread, crusts removed. The croûtons may be made in dices or cut into shapes.

■ COOK'S TIP

If you do not have time to soak the chick peas overnight, cook them, unsoaked, in boiling water for 1 hour and then drain them. Alternatively you may *use canned chick peas, which will not need either soaking or pre-boiling.*

57 CHILLED SHERRIED GRAPEFRUIT

Preparation time:
15 minutes, plus
chilling

Serves 8

Calories:
78 per portion

YOU WILL NEED:
4 grapefruit
100 g/4 oz demerara sugar
4 tablespoons sherry

Halve the grapefruit, loosen the segments with a serrated knife and snip out the core with scissors. Sprinkle 15 g/½ oz of the sugar and ½ tablespoon of the sherry over each half.

Cover the grapefruit halves with cling film and chill for at least 1 hour before serving.

58 GOAT'S CHEESE AND TOMATO HORS D'OEUVRE

Preparation time:
10 minutes

Serves 6

Calories:
297 per portion

YOU WILL NEED:
350 g/12 oz goat's cheese (see Cook's Tip)
½ cucumber, thinly sliced
5-6 large continental tomatoes, sliced
fresh chives or parsley
FOR THE DRESSING
6 tablespoons good flavoured oil, preferably olive oil
3 tablespoons wine vinegar
good pinch of dry mustard
salt and pepper

Cut the cheese into 5 mm/¼ inch slices. On individual plates, arrange the slices of cheese overlapping in a semi-circle round the top half of each plate.

Arrange the cucumber next to the cheese. Overlap the tomato slices around the bottom half of each plate.

To make the dressing, mix or shake the oil, vinegar, mustard, salt and pepper together.

Spoon a little dressing over the tomatoes and arrange the chives or parsley decoratively. Extra vinaigrette can be served separately, if liked.

■ COOK'S TIP

For convenience, this refreshing starter may be prepared several hours before the meal at which it is to be served.

■ COOK'S TIP

Ste Maure is a good variety of goat's cheese to use for this hors d'oeuvre, since it is produced in a cylinder shape which cuts easily into round slices.

59 ARTICHOKES VINAIGRETTE

Preparation time:
10 minutes

Serves 6

Calories:
121 per portion

YOU WILL NEED:
1 x 397 g/14 oz can artichoke hearts
2 hard-boiled eggs
FOR THE DRESSING
4 tablespoons olive oil
1 tablespoon lemon juice
1 teaspoon finely grated lemon rind
1 tablespoon white wine
1 teaspoon clear honey
1 tablespoon each chopped parsley,
    oregano, thyme and basil
1 teaspoon capers, to garnish

Rinse the artichokes under cold running water and drain well. Cut each piece into quarters. Cut the eggs into quarters. Arrange the eggs and artichokes on a serving plate.

Mix all the dressing ingredients together, stirring well so that the herbs are evenly distributed.

Spoon the dressing over the salad and sprinkle with the capers. Cover and chill until required.

60 RATATOUILLE TARTLETS

Preparation time:
25 minutes

Cooking time:
about 35 minutes

Oven temperature:
200 C, 400 F, gas 6

Serves 12

Calories:
188 per portion

YOU WILL NEED:
1 x 400 g/14 oz packet shortcrust
    pastry
FOR THE RATATOUILLE
25 g/1 oz butter
2 garlic cloves, sliced
2 onions, sliced
2 small aubergines, chopped
2 courgettes, sliced
8 tomatoes, skinned, seeded and
    chopped
2 tablespoons tomato purée
salt and pepper
Parmesan cheese (optional)

Roll out the pastry on a floured board and use to line twelve 7.5 cm/3 inch individual flan tins. Prick the bases. Chill for 30 minutes.

Melt the butter in a pan, add the garlic and onions and cook gently for 10 minutes. Stir in the aubergines, courgettes, tomatoes, tomato purée, and salt and pepper to taste. Cover and simmer for 20 minutes.

Line the pastry cases with foil or greaseproof paper and beans and bake in a preheated oven for 12 minutes, until golden brown. Remove the paper and beans and cook for a further 5 minutes.

Spoon the ratatouille into the flan cases and sprinkle with Parmesan, if liked. Serve hot or cold.

■ COOK'S TIP

This herbed vinaigrette dressing, which should be made with fresh herbs, is excellent with many kinds of salad. It gives added interest to green salads.

■ COOK'S TIP

The ratatouille in this recipe would also make a good vegetable accompaniment for steaks and chops. This quantity would serve 4-6; substitute 2-3 tablespoons of a good vegetable oil for the butter in this recipe. Add a seeded and chopped green pepper, if liked.

61 EGG AND WALNUT PATE

Preparation time:
20 minutes, plus
chilling

Cooking time:
5 minutes

Serves 6

Calories:
303 per portion

YOU WILL NEED:

1 small onion, chopped
1-2 garlic cloves, crushed
25 g/1 oz butter or margarine
175 g/6 oz full fat soft cheese
100 g/4 oz shelled walnuts, roughly
    chopped
1 tablespoon chopped fresh parsley
½ teaspoon dried thyme
salt and pepper
2 tablespoons lemon juice
3 eggs, hard-boiled
FOR THE GARNISH
walnut halves
spring onion tassels (see recipe 19)

Fry the onion and garlic gently in the melted fat until soft and lightly browned. Leave to cool.

Soften the cheese in a bowl and beat in the onion mixture followed by the walnuts, parsley, thyme, salt and pepper and lemon juice. Finely grate or chop the eggs and mix evenly through the pâté.

Turn into a dish, level the top and chill until required. Garnish with walnut halves and spring onion tassels, and serve with hot toast or crackers and butter.

62 SMOKED MACKEREL PATE

Preparation time:
15 minutes

Serves 12

Calories:
159 per portion

YOU WILL NEED:

225 g/ 8 oz smoked mackerel
100 g/ 4 oz unsalted butter, softened
    grated rind and juice of half a lemon
2 teaspoons creamed horseradish
salt and pepper
Seeded biscuits (recipe 255), Cheese
    straws (recipe 253), or Melba toast
    (see recipe 63), to serve

Peel off the skin from the mackerel, and flake the flesh. Blend it in a liquidizer or food processor, then gradually work in the butter, lemon juice and rind and the horseradish. Season to taste.

Pile into small bowls and chill well. Serve in the bowls and hand the biscuits separately. Alternatively, pipe the pâté on to biscuits, straws or toast and serve as canapés. Garnish the canapés with cucumber and lemon twists.

■ COOK'S TIP

To make this pâté really
quick and easy to serve,
turn it into individual
ramekin dishes, rather than
one large dish. Garnish each
ramekin dish with a walnut

half and a small sprig of
parsley.

■ COOK'S TIP

This pâté can be made 2 or
3 days before it is required
and stored, tightly covered,
in the refrigerator.

63 TERRINE OF CHICKEN

Preparation time:
20 minutes

Cooking time:
1 hr 25 minutes – 1
hour 40 minutes

Oven temperature:
180 C, 350 F, gas 4

Serves 8

Calories:
229 per portion

YOU WILL NEED:
40 g/1½ oz butter
50 g/2 oz button mushrooms, chopped
1 garlic clove, roughly chopped
450 g/1 lb chicken livers, chopped
3 tablespoons dry red wine
1 teaspoon chopped thyme
salt
1 tablespoon brandy
1 tablespoon single cream
225 g/8 oz boned chicken, thinly sliced
2 tablespoons green peppercorns
lettuce leaves, to garnish

Melt half the butter in a pan, add the mushrooms and cook for 2 minutes. Remove with a slotted spoon and set aside. Add the remaining butter and garlic to the pan; cook for 1 minute. Add the chicken livers and cook for 5 minutes. Add the wine, thyme, and salt to taste. Cook for 15 minutes.

Work the mixture in an electric blender until smooth, then stir in the mushrooms, brandy and cream.

Spoon a thin layer of liver mixture into a lightly greased 450 g/1 lb terrine. Cover with a layer of chicken, then sprinkle with a few peppercorns. Repeat the layers until all the ingredients are used, finishing with the liver mixture. Cover.

Stand the dish in a roasting pan containing enough boiling water to come halfway up the sides of the dish. Cook in a preheated oven for 1-1¼ hours. Cool, then chill until required. Garnish with lettuce and serve with toast.

■ COOK'S TIP

Crispbreads, crackers or Melba toast make interesting changes from ordinary toast for this and other terrines and pâtés. To make Melba toast, toast both sides of a slice of bread, remove the crusts then slice the toast horizontally to make 2 very thin slices. Quickly toast the uncooked sides.

64 SAVOURY CAKE

Preparation time:
15 minutes

Cooking time:
about 1¼ hours

Oven temperature:
150 C, 300 F, gas 2

Makes 36 slices

Total calories: 2081

YOU WILL NEED:
225 g/8 oz lean smoked bacon, chopped
1 large onion, finely chopped
½ teaspoon cayenne pepper
3 teaspoons baking powder
250 g/9 oz plain flour
100 g/4 oz Cheddar cheese, grated
120 ml/4 fl oz oil
325 ml/11 fl oz milk
4 eggs

Grease and line a 20 × 28 × 4 cm/8 × 11 × 1½ inch roasting tin or similar.

In a non-stick pan, lightly fry the bacon and onion until the bacon is crisp. Drain off the fat.

Sift the dry ingredients together into a large bowl and add the cheese. Add the oil, milk and eggs and stir well. Stir in the onion and bacon.

Turn into the prepared tin. Bake in the preheated oven for about 1 hour 10 minutes until set and browned.

■ COOK'S TIP

This savoury cake may be served either hot or cold, cut into slices. Serve it with a green salad or the Tomato and leek salad (recipe 79).

65 CURRIED PRAWN RING

Preparation time:
20 minutes

Cooking time:
about 22 minutes

Serves 6

Calories:
403 per portion

YOU WILL NEED:
350 g/12 oz long-grain rice
few saffron threads
1 tablespoon sunflower oil
1 tablespoon curry powder
8 spring onions, chopped
1 red pepper, seeded and chopped
50 g/2 oz pine nuts
75 g/3 oz sultanas
225 g/8 oz peeled prawns
FOR THE DRESSING
4 tablespoons olive oil
2 tablespoons white wine vinegar
1 teaspoon dry mustard
1 teaspoon sugar
2 tablespoons chopped coriander

Cook the rice in boiling salted water, with the saffron added, for about 20 minutes, until the rice is tender and much of the liquid absorbed. Meanwhile, place the dressing ingredients in a screw-top jar and shake well to blend.

Drain the rice well, place in a bowl and stir in the dressing while still warm. Set aside to cool slightly.

Heat the oil in a pan, add the curry powder, spring onions, red pepper, pine nuts and sultanas and cook, stirring, for 1½ minutes. Add to the rice and leave until completely cold.

Stir in the prawns, then spoon the mixture into a lightly oiled 1.5 litre/2½ pint ring mould, pressing down well. Chill until required. To serve, invert the ring on to a serving plate.

■ COOK'S TIP

Use a standard metal ring mould for this recipe, oiling the inside with a light, little-flavoured oil, such as arachide (peanut) or sunflower.

66 MEDITERRANEAN SEAFOOD

Preparation time:
15 minutes

Cooking time:
20-22 minutes

Serves 4

Calories:
424 per portion

YOU WILL NEED:
15 g/½ oz butter
2 shallots, chopped
150 ml/¼ pint dry white wine
2 tablespoons dry sherry
1 teaspoon French mustard
pinch of cayenne
dash of Worcestershire sauce
150 ml/¼ pint double cream
2 × 177 g/6 oz cans crabmeat, drained
225 g/8 oz peeled prawns
salt and pepper
2-3 tablespoons grated Parmesan
    cheese

Melt the butter in a pan, add the shallots and cook until softened, without browning. Pour in the wine and sherry, bring to the boil and boil rapidly until thickened and reduced by half.

Stir in the mustard, cayenne and Worcestershire sauce and cook for 2 minutes. Add the cream, bring to the boil, and boil for 5-7 minutes, stirring occasionally, until thickened.

Remove from the heat, stir in the fish and season with salt and pepper to taste.

Sprinkle with the cheese and serve immediately. Garnish with lime slices and herbs if liked.

■ COOK'S TIP

Rice or new potatoes, and a tossed mixed salad make good accompaniments for this dish.

67 STIR-FRIED FISH WITH VEGETABLES

Preparation time:
20 minutes, plus
salting time

Cooking time:
about 20 minutes

Serves 4

Calories:
174 per portion

YOU WILL NEED:
*450 g/1 lb cod fillet, skinned and cut
    into 2.5 cm/1 inch wide strips*
1 teaspoon salt
1 tablespoon oil
*2 rashers rindless back bacon,
    shredded*
50 g/2 oz frozen peas, cooked
50 g/2 oz frozen sweetcorn, cooked
6 tablespoons chicken stock or water
2 teaspoons dry sherry
*2 teaspoons soy sauce (see Cook's
    Tip)*
1 teaspoon sugar
1 teaspoon cornflour
1 teaspoon water
*spring onion tassels, to garnish (see
    recipe 19)*

Sprinkle the fish fillets with the salt and leave for 15 minutes.

Heat the oil in a frying pan or a wok, add the fish and bacon and stir-fry for 3 minutes. Add the remaining ingredients, except the cornflour and 1 teaspoon water, and bring to the boil. Blend the cornflour and water and stir in. Cook for 1 minute.

Garnish with spring onion tassels and serve immediately.

68 CREOLE-STYLE PRAWNS

Preparation time:
15 minutes

Cooking time:
30 minutes

Serves 6

Calories:
123 per portion

YOU WILL NEED:
1 tablespoon oil
1 large onion, chopped
1 garlic clove, crushed
2 celery sticks, thinly sliced
350 g/12 oz tomatoes, skinned
1 green pepper, cored and seeded
salt and pepper
4 tablespoons dry white wine
1 tablespoon tomato purée
450 g/1 lb peeled prawns
2 drops Tabasco sauce
1 teaspoon Worcestershire sauce
1 tablespoon chopped parsley

Heat the oil in a pan, add the onion and garlic and fry until lightly browned. Add the celery and cook for 2 minutes.

Cut the tomatoes in half, remove the seeds and chop the flesh. Finely chop the green pepper. Add the tomatoes and pepper to the pan with salt and pepper to taste. Stir in the wine and tomato purée. Bring to the boil and simmer, uncovered, for 20 minutes.

Stir in the prawns, Tabasco and Worcestershire sauces. Simmer for 5 minutes, then stir in the parsley. Serve the prawns immediately, garnished with lemon twists and celery leaves, if liked.

COOK'S TIP

*Use the common dark
variety of soy sauce, widely
available in supermarkets,
in this recipe. Light soy
sauce is often used as an
accompaniment.*

COOK'S TIP

*To make a satisfying main
course of these spicy
prawns, serve them with
plain rice or pasta and a
green salad.*

69 MONKFISH AND SCALLOP CASSEROLE

Preparation time:
20 minutes

Cooking time:
about 50 minutes

Oven temperature
160 C, 325 F, gas 3

Serves 6

Calories:
207 per portion

YOU WILL NEED:
40 g/1½ oz butter or margarine
1 onion, sliced
1 celery stick, sliced
1 large carrot, diced
1-2 garlic cloves, crushed
500 g/1¼ lb monkfish
350 g/12 oz prepared scallops
1 × 425 g/15 oz can tomatoes
1 tablespoon tomato purée
½ teaspoon Worcestershire sauce
1 tablespoon lemon juice
150 ml/¼ pint dry white wine
salt and pepper
good pinch of ground coriander
1 bay leaf
1 tablespoon cornflour

Melt the fat in a flameproof casserole and fry the onion, celery, carrot and garlic gently until soft, stirring occasionally.

Skin the monkfish and cut it into 2 cm/¾ inch cubes. Halve or quarter the scallops, depending on their size. Add the fish to the casserole and continue cooking for 2-3 minutes.

Add the can of tomatoes, tomato purée, Worcestershire sauce, lemon juice, wine, salt and pepper, coriander and the bay leaf and bring to the boil. Cover the casserole tightly and cook in a preheated oven for 40 minutes.

Blend the cornflour with a little cold water, add it to the casserole, and bring back to the boil for a minute or so.

■ COOK'S TIP

Monkfish, also called Angler fish, has a firm, white and succulent flesh which makes it ideal for this casserole.

70 MACARONI AND TUNA FISH LAYER

Preparation time:
25 minutes

Cooking time:
about 50 minutes

Oven temperature:
220 C, 425 F, gas 7

Serves 6

Calories:
479 per portion

YOU WILL NEED:
40 g/1½ or butter
1 large onion, sliced
1 garlic clove, crushed
100 g/4 oz mushrooms, chopped
1 teaspoon dried majoram
2 × 200 g/7 oz cans tuna fish in brine, drained and flaked
4-6 tablespoons natural yogurt
salt and pepper
350 g/12 oz short-cut macaroni, cooked
600 ml/1 pint cheese sauce (see Cook's Tip)
2-3 tomatoes, peeled and sliced
25 g/1 oz Cheddar cheese, grated
2 tablespoons grated Parmesan cheese

Melt the butter in a pan and fry the onion and garlic gently until soft. Add the mushrooms and continue frying for a few minutes. Stir in the majoram, tuna fish and yogurt and heat through until really hot. Season well.

Put half the macaroni into a greased ovenproof dish. Spoon the tuna fish mixture in an even layer over the macaroni and cover with the remaining macaroni.

Make the sauce (see Cook's Tip) and pour it over the macaroni. Cover with sliced tomatoes, then sprinkle with the cheeses. Cook in a preheated oven for 25-30 minutes until golden brown and bubbling.

■ COOK'S TIP

For the sauce, make a roux with 50 g/2 oz butter and 3 tablespoons plain flour. Add 600 ml/1 pint milk or stock and bring slowly to the boil. Add 1 teaspoon dry mustard and pepper to taste. Simmer 2 minutes, remove from heat and add 50 g/2 oz grated Cheddar cheese and 1 tablespoon Parmesan. Stir until melted.

71 CHICKEN IN SESAME SAUCE

Preparation time:
15 minutes, plus
marinating

Cooking time:
about 10 minutes

Serves 4

Calories:
488 per portion

YOU WILL NEED:
450 g/1 lb boneless chicken breast, cut
   into cubes
1 tablespoon oil
100 g/4 oz unsalted cashew nuts
75 g/3 oz canned straw mushrooms,
   drained and halved
FOR THE MARINADE
3 spring onions, chopped
3 tablespoons dark soy sauce
2 tablespoons hot pepper oil
2 tablespoons sesame seed oil
1 tablespoon sesame seed paste
1 teaspoon ground Szechuan
   peppercorns

Put the marinade ingredients into a bowl. Add the chicken cubes, turning to coat thoroughly. Leave to marinate for 30 minutes.

Meanwhile, heat the oil in a wok or frying pan, add the cashew nuts and fry until golden brown. Drain on kitchen paper.

Add the chicken and marinade to the pan and stir-fry for 2 minutes. Add the mushrooms to the pan. Cook for a further minute. Pile the mixture on to a warmed serving dish and sprinkle with the nuts. Serve immediately.

72 CHICKEN CLAMITANO

Preparation time:
10 minutes

Cooking time:
about 40 minutes

Serves 4

Calories:
388 per portion

YOU WILL NEED:
16 chicken wings
1 × 284 ml/10 fl oz can tomato and
   clam juice
3-4 shakes Tabasco sauce
150 ml/¼ pint water
2 bay leaves
12-16 black olives
salt and pepper
parsley, to garnish

Put all the ingredients, except salt and pepper, into a pan and simmer, uncovered, for 35 minutes or until the chicken is very tender and the sauce has reduced slightly. Season with salt and pepper to taste, remembering to allow for the saltiness of the olives.

Garnish with parsley and serve with crisply cooked green beans.

■ COOK'S TIP

Chicken has been a common ingredient in oriental cooking for thousands of years, and this receipe makes full use of exotic ingredients to enhance the flavour. Hot pepper oil contains chillies, so if it is not available, use plain oil and add crushed chillies to taste (half a teaspoonful should be sufficient).

■ COOK'S TIP

Other small cuts of chicken, such as drumsticks or thighs, will work well in this recipe.

73 FETTUCINE IN FOUR CHEESES

Preparation time:
15 minutes

Cooking time:
about 25 minutes

Serves 4

Calories:
726 per portion

YOU WILL NEED:
450 g/1 lb fettucine
salt
2 tablespoons oil
1 onion
2 garlic cloves
FOR THE SAUCE
25 g/1 oz butter
2 garlic cloves, sliced
50 g/2 oz Emmental cheese, grated
50 g/2 oz Bel Paese cheese, grated
50 g/2 oz Parmesan cheese, grated
50 g/2 oz Cheddar cheese, grated
175 ml/6 fl oz single cream
salt and pepper
FOR THE GARNISH
1 tablespoon chopped basil
1 tablespoon chopped parsley

Put the pasta, salt, oil, onion, and garlic in a large pan of boiling water and cook for 8–9 minutes, until the pasta is just cooked.

Meanwhile, make the sauce. Melt the butter in a pan, add the garlic and cook, without browning, for 3 minutes. Stir in the cheeses and cream and continue stirring over a low heat until the cheeses have melted. Season with salt and pepper to taste.

Drain the pasta and remove the onion and garlic. Toss the pasta in the sauce, sprinkle with the herbs and serve.

■ COOK'S TIP

Tagliatelle may be used instead of the fettucine in this recipe, if liked. A tomato and onion salad makes a good accompaniment.

74 CREOLE SPICED BEEF

Preparation time:
30 minutes, plus
marinating

Cooking time:
about 2¼ hours

Oven temperature:
150 C, 300 F, gas 2

Serves 6

Calories:
421 per portion

YOU WILL NEED:
1.25 kg/2½ lb braising steak
juice of 2 limes
4 garlic cloves, crushed
2 teaspoons ground cinnamon
¼ teaspoon ground cloves
2 teaspoons grated fresh ginger
1 green chilli, seeded and chopped
1½ teaspoons salt
3 tablespoons oil or dripping
3 bay leaves
½ teaspoon ground nutmeg
2 tablespoons dark rum
3 tablespoons water
2 teaspoons annatto liquid
freshly ground black pepper
fresh coriander leaves, to garnish

Cut the beef into 4 cm/1½ inch cubes and place them in a shallow dish. Combine the lime juice, the garlic, cinnamon, ground cloves, ginger, chilli and salt. Pour over the beef, mix thoroughly, cover securely and leave to marinate for 24-28 hours, turning the beef several times.

Heat the oil or dripping in a flameproof casserole and add the beef and all the marinade. Fry gently for 10 minutes, stirring frequently. Add the bay leaves, nutmeg, rum, water and annatto, season with pepper and bring to the boil.

Cover the casserole tightly and cook in a preheated oven for 2 hours, stirring the beef once during cooking. Serve garnished with coriander.

■ COOK'S TIP

Annatto is the seed of a tree native to Central America and the West Indies. It is best known as a colouring agent, but the crushed seed is sometimes used as a spice.

As the flavour is very delicate, orange food colouring can be used instead.

75 PORK CHOPS WITH JUNIPER

Preparation time:
10 minutes

Cooking time:
30 minutes

Serves 4

Calories:
687 per portion

YOU WILL NEED:
4 tablespoons olive oil
4 pork chops, about 225 g/8 oz each
2 shallots, chopped
1 garlic clove, chopped
8 juniper berries, roughly crushed
225 g/8 oz tomatoes, skinned and
   roughly chopped
4 tablespoons gin or vodka
120 ml/4 fl oz chicken stock
½ tablespoon chopped fresh thyme
salt and pepper
fresh thyme, to garnish

Heat the oil in a deep frying pan with a lid. Add tne pork chops and fry over a brisk heat for 3-4 minutes on each side to brown, then remove and keep warm. Add the shallots to the pan and fry over a gentle heat for 2 minutes, then add the garlic and cook for 1 further minute.

Stir in the juniper berries and tomatoes and cook for 2-3 minutes, stirring. Then add the gin or vodka and boil rapidly over a brisk heat until reduced by half. Pour in the stock and stir in the thyme. Season to taste with salt and pepper.

Return the pork chops to the pan, cover and simmer for 15-20 minutes, adding a little extra stock if necessary, until the chops are cooked through. Serve garnished with fresh thyme.

76 PAN-FRIED CALVES' LIVER WITH THYME

Preparation time:
10 minutes

Cooking time:
about 10 minutes

Serves 2

Calories:
405 per portion

YOU WILL NEED:
2 slices calves' liver, about 75-100 g/
   3-4 oz each or 4 very thin slices
2 tablespoons seasoned flour
40 g/1½ oz butter or margarine
¼ level teaspoon dried thyme or ½
   teaspoon freshly chopped thyme
3 tablespoons dry sherry
grated rind of ½ lime or lemon
1 tablespoon lime or lemon juice
salt and pepper
FOR THE GARNISH
slices of lime or lemon
sprigs of fresh thyme

If the liver is thick, cut each piece carefully into two thinner slices. Toss the liver in the seasoned flour.

Melt the fat in a frying pan, add the thyme and then the liver. Fry gently for 2-4 minutes on each side until well sealed and just cooked through, but in no way overcooked. Transfer to 2 plates and keep warm.

Add the sherry to the pan juices, followed by the lime rind and juice. Heat gently until it bubbles well. Taste and adjust the seasoning and pour over the liver.

Garnish with slices of lime and sprigs of thyme placed beside the liver.

■ COOK'S TIP

Juniper berries are the fruit of an evergreen shrub, Juniper communis, *native to the northern hemisphere. Usually sold dried, they are used to flavour gin, game* and pork. Their special affinity with pork, adding a deliciously spicy flavour, explains their use in many pork-based dishes, including pâtés.

■ COOK'S TIP

This recipe works well with the less expensive lamb's liver. Ensure the slices are thin and cook them very gently.

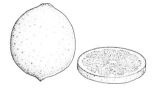

77 STUFFED PANCAKES

Preparation time:
25 minutes

Cooking time:
about 45 minutes

Oven temperature:
200 C, 400 F, gas 6

Serves 4

Calories:
440 per portion

YOU WILL NEED:
100 g/4 oz plain flour
¼ teaspoon salt
2 small eggs
1 tablespoon oil
150 ml/¼ pint milk
6 tablespoons water
225 g/8 oz chopped spinach, cooked
225 g/8 oz Ricotta or curd cheese
25 g/1 oz grated Parmesan cheese
1 egg, beaten
grated nutmeg
salt and pepper
25 g/1 oz butter
3 tablespoons grated Parmesan cheese
5 tablespoons chicken stock

For the pancakes, sift the flour and salt into a bowl. Make a well in the centre and add the eggs, oil and milk. Beat until smooth, then stir in the water. Cover and chill for 1-2 hours.

Lightly oil an 18 cm/7 inch frying pan and place over moderate heat. When hot, pour in just enough batter to cover the base. When the pancake is set and the underside lightly browned, turn and briefly cook the other side. Repeat with the remaining batter, making 8 pancakes in all.

For the filling, squeeze the spinach dry, then mix it with the cheeses, egg, nutmeg and seasoning. Divide between the pancakes, roll up and arrange in a buttered ovenproof dish. Dot with butter, sprinkle with the Parmesan and pour in the stock. Bake in a preheated oven for 20 minutes until golden.

◾ COOK'S TIP

These filled pancakes may be prepared in advance to the filled and rolled stage, and kept covered in the refrigerator until required. Add the butter, parmesan *and stock to the dish of pancakes before baking them.*

78 OMELETTE WITH MEAT SAUCE

Preparation time:
15 minutes

Cooking time:
about 20 minutes

Serves 4

Calories:
373 per portion

YOU WILL NEED:
3 tablespoons oil
1 garlic clove, crushed
2 spring onions, finely chopped
2 celery sticks, chopped
1 boneless chicken breast, diced
100 g/4 oz minced pork
2 teaspoons cornflour
1 tablespoon water
1 tablespoon dry sherry
2 tablespoons soy sauce
6 eggs, beaten
salt and pepper
FOR THE GARNISH
spring onions
celery leaves

Heat 1 tablespoon of the oil in a wok or frying pan, add the garlic, spring onions and celery and cook for 1 minute. Increase the heat, add the meats and cook for 2 minutes.

Blend the cornflour with the water. Stir into the sauce with the sherry and soy sauce and simmer, stirring occasionally, for 15 minutes.

Meanwhile, make the omelette. Season the eggs with salt and pepper to taste. Heat the remaining 2 tablespoons oil in a large frying pan, pour in the eggs and cook gently, drawing the cooked edges towards the centre with a fork, until set.

Carefully transfer to a warmed serving dish. Spoon over the meat sauce and garnish with spring onions and celery.

◾ COOK'S TIP

For an authentic Chinese flavour, substitute Chinese rice wine for the dry sherry in this recipe.

79 TOMATO AND LEEK SALAD

Preparation time:
15 minutes

Serves 4

Calories:
294 per portion

YOU WILL NEED:
450 g/1 lb tomatoes, sliced
100 g/4 oz leeks, thinly sliced
4 tablespoons honey and lemon dressing (see recipe 13)
1 tablespoon chopped parsley, to garnish

Arrange the tomatoes and leeks in layers in a shallow serving dish, finishing with leeks. Pour over the dressing and sprinkle with the parsley.

80 COURGETTE AND TOMATO SALAD

Preparation time:
10 minutes, plus marinating

Serves 6

Calories:
281 per portion

YOU WILL NEED:
225 g/8 oz courgettes, very thinly sliced (see Cook's Tip)
6 small tomatoes, sliced
50 g/2 oz black olives, halved and stoned
1 tablespoon chopped marjoram
1 tablespoon chopped parsley
FOR THE DRESSING
175 ml/6 fl oz olive oil
4 tablespoons wine vinegar
1 teaspoon French mustard
4 garlic cloves, crushed
1 teaspoon clear honey
salt and pepper

First, make the dressing. Put all the ingredients in a screw-top jar and shake well to mix. The ingredients here make 250 ml/8 fl oz, so there will be some left over; it will keep in the refrigerator for 2 or 3 weeks.

Place the courgettes in a bowl, pour over 6 tablespoons of the dressing and leave to marinate overnight.

Add the remaining ingredients, toss thoroughly and turn into a salad bowl.

■ COOK'S TIP

The leeks may be marinated in the dressing for 15 minutes before combining with the tomatoes if a more mellow flavour is preferred.

■ COOK'S TIP

The very small, young courgettes are the most suitable to use raw in salads. Slice them thinly to allow the flavour of the dressing to be absorbed.

81 PRALINE PEACH GATEAU

Preparation time:
20 minutes

Cooking time:
30-35 minutes

Oven temperature:
190 C, 375 F, gas 5

Serves 6

Calories:
604 per portion

YOU WILL NEED:
3 eggs
150 g/5 oz caster sugar
grated rind of 1 lemon
75 g/3 oz plain flour, sifted
1 × recipe praline (see recipe 50)
300 ml/½ pint double cream, whipped
4 tablespoons apricot jam
2 teaspoons water
2 peaches, stoned and sliced

Place the eggs, sugar and lemon rind in a bowl and whisk with an electric mixer until thick and mousse-like. Carefully fold in the flour, then turn into a lined, greased and floured deep 20 cm/8 inch cake tin.

Bake in a preheated oven for 30-35 minutes, until the cake springs back when lightly pressed. Turn on to a wire rack to cool.

Make the praline as for Praline Charlotte (recipe 50) and fold half into two thirds of the cream. Split the cake in half and sandwich together with the praline cream.

Heat the jam with the water, sieve, reheat and use three quarters to glaze the side of the cake. Press the remaining praline around the side.

Arrange the peaches, overlapping, in a circle on top, leaving a border around the edge. Reheat the remaining glaze and brush it over the peaches. Pipe the remaining cream in a decorative border around the edge.

82 CREME BRULEE

Preparation time:
10 minutes

Cooking time:
about 30 minutes

Oven temperature:
160 C, 325 F, gas 3

Serves 4

Calories:
459 per portion

YOU WILL NEED:
300 ml/½ pint double cream
12 drops vanilla essence
2 egg yolks
100 g/4 oz caster sugar

Place the cream and vanilla essence in a small pan and heat very gently. Whisk the egg yolks with 2 teaspoons of the sugar in a heatproof basin. Stir in the cream and stand the basin over a pan of simmering water. Stir constantly until the mixture thickens slightly.

Pour into 4 ramekin dishes and bake in a preheated oven for 8 minutes. Cool slightly, then place in the refrigerator until thoroughly chilled, preferably overnight.

Sprinkle evenly with the remaining sugar and place under a preheated hot grill until the sugar has caramelized. Cool, then chill for about 2 hours before serving.

■ COOK'S TIP

When whipping cream for piping, whip it until it is only just stiff; any more and it may turn buttery as the cream will thicken further, from the warmth of the hands on the piping bag, when it is being piped.

■ COOK'S TIP

Demerara sugar may be used for the caramelized topping instead of caster sugar. It gives a good colour and a really crisp topping.

83 CINNAMON CHEESECAKE WITH KIWI FRUIT

Preparation time:
40 minutes, plus chilling

Cooking time:
about 5 minutes

Serves 10

Calories:
443 per portion

YOU WILL NEED:
400 g/14 oz full fat soft cheese
½ teaspoon ground cinnamon
150 ml/¼ pint soured cream
grated rind of 1 lemon
50 g/2 oz caster sugar
2 tablespoons lemon juice
1 tablespoon water
15 g/½ oz powdered gelatine
75 g/3 oz butter
225 g/8 oz digestive biscuits, crushed
25 g/1 oz unsalted peanuts, chopped
1 kiwi fruit, peeled and sliced
fresh mint, to decorate

Line a 23 × 13 cm/9 × 5 inch loaf tin with non-stick silicone paper. Beat the cream cheese until it is soft, then beat in the cinnamon, soured cream, lemon rind and sugar.

Put the lemon juice and water into a small bowl, sprinkle over the gelatine and heat over a pan of gently simmering water until the gelatine dissolves. Leave to cool a little, then mix evenly through the cream cheese mixture. Pour into the tin and chill until almost set.

Heat the butter gently in a saucepan until it has melted. Stir in the crushed biscuits and chopped nuts and mix until evenly blended. Spoon the mixture in an even layer over the cheesecake. Press down lightly and chill until firm.

Turn out the cheesecake on to a plate and peel off the paper. Decorate with slices of kiwi fruit and mint leaves.

84 GUAVA AND MANDARIN SYLLABUBS

Preparation time:
15 minutes, plus standing

Serves 6

Calories:
337 per portion

YOU WILL NEED:
1 × 425 g/15 oz can guavas
1 × 300 g/11 oz can mandarin oranges
grated rind of 1 lemon
4 tablespoons lemon juice
100 g/4 oz caster sugar
2 tablespoons brandy
2 tablespoons sherry
300 ml/½ pint double cream
4 tablespoons natural yogurt (optional)

Drain the guavas and roughly chop; drain the mandarins and put 18 aside for decoration, if wished. Mix the remainder with the guavas and divide between 6 wine glasses.

Make the syllabub. Put the lemon rind, juice, sugar, brandy and sherry into a bowl and, if you have the time, leave it to stand for at least 15 minutes and up to 1 hour.

Add the cream to the mixture and whip until it is thick and stands in soft peaks. Add the yogurt, if using, and continue to whip until it is completely mixed in.

Spoon or pipe the syllabub over the fruit in the glasses and decorate each one with 3 mandarin orange segments if wished. Serve within an hour, or chill and serve within 2 or 3 hours.

▪ COOK'S TIP

Serve this cheesecake cut in slices on individual plates. Allowing guests to help themselves could result in a very messy cheesecake!

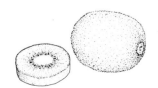

▪ COOK'S TIP

Any type of canned fruit can be used for this dessert, depending on what is available in the store cupboard. Alternatively, used sliced fresh bananas, *grapes, oranges or crushed biscuits in the base. The brandy and sherry may be replaced with sweet white wine, if liked.*

85 SPICED APPLES

Preparation time:
10 minutes

Cooking time:
about 1 hour

Oven temperature:
150 C, 300 F, gas 2

Serves 6

Calories:
145 per portion

YOU WILL NEED:
6 dessert apples
6 cloves
450 ml/¾ pint dry cider
juice and thinly pared rind of 1 lime
100 g/4 oz caster sugar

Peel and core the apples. Cut each into six segments.

Put the rest of the ingredients into a 1.5 litre (2½ pint) casserole. Stir to dissolve the sugar, then add the apples, stir and cover.

Put the casserole in a preheated oven and bake for about 1 hour or until the apples are tender (the time depends on the type of apples used). Remove the lime rind and cloves. Serve hot or cold.

86 STUFFED PINEAPPLE

Preparation time:
15 minutes

Serves 6

Calories:
93 per portion

YOU WILL NEED:
1 large pineapple
2 tablespoons caster sugar
1 tablespoon Curacao
2 tablespoons rum
juice of 1-2 passion fruits
1 ripe mango, peeled, stoned and cubed
1 ripe pawpaw or papaya, peeled, seeded and cubed
juice of 1 lime
lime quarters, to decorate

Cut the pineapple in half lengthways. Using a small knife, carefully remove the flesh and cut it into cubes, discarding the core.

Combine the sugar, Curacao, rum and passion fruit juice in a bowl. Add the mango, pawpaw and pineapple to the liqueur mixture and toss well together.

Spoon the fruit into the pineapple halves, piling it well up and pour the juice overall. Decorate with lime quarters to serve.

■ COOK'S TIP

Serve these refreshingly simple apples on their own after a rich main course or to finish a light supper. Thick pouring cream would make this a luxury dessert.

■ COOK'S TIP

A good, non-fruit, ice cream, such as vanilla or coconut, makes an excellent accompaniment for this fruit dessert.

87 PEACH AND PASSION FRUIT CHANTILLY

Preparation time:
15 minutes

Serves 4

Calories:
187 per portion

YOU WILL NEED:
3 passion fruit
6 peaches, skinned, halved and stoned
120 ml/4 fl oz double cream
2 tablespoons orange flower water (optional)

Cut the passion fruit in half using a sharp knife, and scoop out the flesh into a bowl. Slice the peaches thinly and add to the bowl. Carefully toss the fruit together until combined and spoon into 4 individual glasses or serving dishes.

Whip the cream together with the orange flower water, if using, until it stands in soft peaks. Spoon a little cream on to each fruit salad before serving.

88 NECTARINES IN GRAND MARNIER

Preparation time:
30 minutes, plus chilling

Cooking time:
about 10 minutes

Serves 2

Calories:
354 per portion

YOU WILL NEED:
3-4 ripe nectarines or peaches (see Cook's Tip)
250 ml/8 fl oz water
2 pieces thinly pared lemon rind
2 pieces thinly pared orange rind
100 g/4 oz caster sugar
4 tablespoons Grand Marnier

Quarter the fruit and remove the stones. Place in a bowl. They may be left whole but it is more difficult to flavour the whole fruit quickly.

Put the water, lemon and orange rind and sugar into a saucepan and heat gently until the sugar dissolves, then boil hard until reduced by just over a third. Remove from the heat and stir in the Grand Marnier.

Pour the syrup over the nectarines (or peaches), cover and chill for at least 12 hours and up to 36 hours, turning the fruit once or twice.

Remove the pieces of orange and lemon rind and cut into julienne strips. Divide the fruit and juice between 2 glass dishes and sprinkle with a little of the strips of citrus rind. Serve as they are or with cream.

◼ COOK'S TIP

Passion fruit are ready to eat when their skins are dimpled. The whole flesh, including the pips, may be eaten.

◼ COOK'S TIP

Nectarines will not need to be peeled for this recipe, but peaches will. To peel peaches, dip them briefly in boiling water, then plunge them into cold water to *loosen the skins. Make a small cut in the skin and peel it off.*

OUTDOOR PARTIES

Informal entertaining, either in the garden or at a picnic, has become an essential part of summer living. The recipes in this chapter include dishes to be cooked on the barbecue, food which can be packed for picnics and some delectable desserts to enjoy in the open air.

89 BARBECUED BONED LEG OF LAMB

Preparation time:
15 minutes, plus marinating

Cooking time:
1½ hours

Serves 6

Calories:
866 per portion

YOU WILL NEED:
1 × 1.5 kg/3 lb lean leg of lamb, boned
4 tablespoons oil
2 tablespoons wine vinegar
salt and pepper
1 garlic clove, crushed
Creole Sauce, hot (recipe 122)

Flatten the lamb with a cutlet bat or a rolling pin. Put in a shallow dish. Mix together the oil, vinegar, seasoning and garlic and pour over the lamb. Marinate in the refrigerator for at least 2 hours.

Place the meat on the greased grill of a preheated barbecue and cook for about 1½ hours, turning every 10-15 minutes. Brush with the Creole sauce towards the end of the cooking.

90 SOUVLAKIA

Preparation time:
25 minutes, plus chilling

Cooking time:
10 minutes

Serves 4

Calories:
570 per portion

YOU WILL NEED:
1 kg/2¼ lb lean lamb, cut into 4 cm/1½ inch cubes
6 tablespoons olive oil
4 tablespoons lemon juice
2 large garlic cloves, crushed
1 tablespoon chopped fresh oregano
1 tablespoon chopped fresh thyme
1 tablespoon chopped fresh marjoram
salt and pepper
100 g/4 oz Feta cheese, crumbled
4 bay leaves, crumbled (optional)

Trim any fat or sinew from the lamb cubes and put them in a shallow dish. Mix the olive oil with the lemon juice, garlic, chopped herbs and seasoning to taste. Spoon this marinade evenly over the lamb. Cover the dish and chill for at least 4 hours.

Remove the lamb cubes and drain, reserving the marinade. Thread the cubes on to 4 kebab skewers and brush with some of the marinade. Cook on the greased grill of a preheated barbecue for about 5 minutes on each side.

Sprinkle the kebabs with the crumbled Feta cheese (and the crumbled bay leaves, if liked). Serve immediately with hot pitta bread and a vegetable dish such as Courgettes à la Grecque (recipe 114).

■ COOK'S TIP

When flattening any meat, dip the cutlet bat or rolling pin in cold water frequently to prevent it sticking to the flesh.

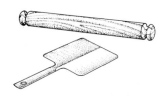

■ COOK'S TIP

As Feta cheese is distinctively salty, remember to use very little salt in the marinade. If liked, split the hot pitta bread and spread the inside with garlic butter.

91 KOREAN KEBABS

Preparation time:
25 minutes, plus
marinating

Cooking time:
10-15 minutes

Serves 4

Calories:
404 per portion

YOU WILL NEED:
1 large garlic clove, crushed
4 tablespoons soy sauce
4 tablespoons oil
2 tablespoons peanut butter
2 tablespoons finely chopped spring
  onion
1 teaspoon sesame seeds
salt and pepper
pinch of chilli powder
750 g/1½ lb lean lamb, cut into
  1 cm/½ inch cubes

Put the garlic, soy sauce, oil and peanut butter in a bowl and
whisk well. Gradually whisk in the spring onion, sesame
seeds, seasoning and chilli powder. Add the meat and turn to
coat. Marinate in the refrigerator for 2-4 hours.

Thread the meat on to small skewers and cook on the
greased grill of a preheated barbecue for 10-15 minutes.

92 LAMB PATTIES

Preparation time:
15 minutes, plus
chilling

Cooking time:
20 minutes

Serves 4

Calories:
346 per portion

YOU WILL NEED:
750 g/1½ lb finely minced lean lamb
salt and pepper
1 tablespoon chopped fresh mint or 2
  teaspoons dried mint
2 tablespoons milk
8 rashers rindless streaky bacon

Mix the lamb with the seasoning, mint and milk. Divide the
mixture in 8 square patties. Chill for 1 hour.

Wrap the bacon around the patties and secure firmly with
a small skewer. Cook on the greased grill of a preheated barbecue for about 20 minutes, turning once.

■ COOK'S TIP

Salt-free peanut butter is
available from health food
shops. Use either smooth or
crunchy peanut butter for
the marinade. Use either
light or dark soy sauce.

■ COOK'S TIP

The easiest way of removing
the rinds from bacon
rashers is with a pair of
kitchen scissors. The rinds
can be used to flavour soup
made with pulses.

93 QUODBAN

Preparation time:
25 minutes, plus
chilling

Cooking time:
5-8 minutes

Serves 4

Calories:
532 per portion

YOU WILL NEED:
750 g/1½ lb lamb fillet
2 tablespoons lemon juice
150 ml/¼ pint olive oil
2 teaspoons crushed coriander seeds
2 garlic cloves, crushed
2 teaspoons ground turmeric
1 teaspoon ground ginger
2 teaspoons ground cumin
2 bay leaves, crumbled
salt and pepper
2 limes, cut into thin wedges

Trim off any fat or sinew from the lamb and cut it into 2.5 cm/1 inch cubes. Put the cubed meat into a shallow dish. Mix the lemon juice with the olive oil, coriander seeds, garlic, turmeric, ginger, cumin, bay leaves and seasoning to taste. Pour this marinade over the meat and stir well. Cover the meat and chill for 12 hours, turning the cubes once or twice.

Remove the meat and drain, reserving the marinade. Thread the cubes of meat on to 4 kebab skewers, threading wedges of lime in between some of the cubes. Brush each kebab with some of the marinade. Cook the kebabs on the greased grill of a preheated barbecue for 5-8 minutes, until the meat is cooked. Serve the kebabs with hot pitta bread.

94 MECHOUI

Preparation time:
15 minutes, plus
chilling

Cooking time:
35-50 minutes (see
recipe)

Serves 6

Calories:
587 per portion

YOU WILL NEED:
1 × 2 kg/4½ lb leg of lamb
FOR THE MARINADE
150 ml/¼ pint olive oil
1 tablespoon chopped fresh marjoram
2 tablespoons chopped fresh mint
½ teaspoon ground cinnamon
½ teaspoon ground cloves
2 garlic cloves, crushed
salt and pepper
2 tablespoons rosewater (see Cook's Tip)

Make several deep widthways cuts at regular intervals in the lamb. Put the lamb into a shallow dish. Mix the marinade ingredients (except the rosewater) together and spoon over the lamb; cover and chill for at least 6 hours, turning occasionally.

Remove the lamb from its marinade and drain, reserving the marinade. Fix the joint securely on to a spit and brush all over lightly with the marinade. Spit-roast over a preheated barbecue, sprinkling with the rosewater occasionally, for about 35-45 minutes until the lamb is sufficiently cooked to carve off the outer slices. Leave the rest of the lamb on the spit and carve off slices as they are ready.

Serve the lamb with warm pitta bread and a cucumber and yogurt salad.

■ COOK'S TIP

The kebabs can be prepared in advance, covered with foil and left to marinate in the refrigerator for up to 24 hours. If limes are unavailable, use lemons.

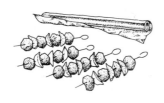

■ COOK'S TIP

To make rosewater, simmer 225 g/8 oz unblemished red rose petals in a pan with 450 ml/¾ pint water for about 30 minutes until the petals are limp. Strain the
liquid into a clean pan, add 75 g/3 oz caster sugar and stir until dissolved. Simmer for 5 minutes, then cool. Store in the refrigerator for up to 2 weeks.

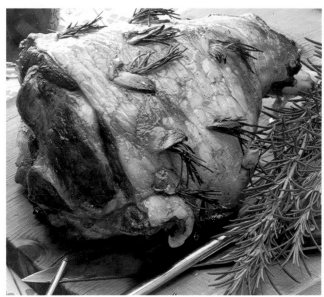

95 LAMBURGERS

Preparation time:
15 minutes, plus
chilling

Cooking time:
15 minutes

Serves 4

Calories:
236 per portion

YOU WILL NEED:
575 g/1¼ lb finely minced lamb
2 tablespoons oil
1 large garlic clove, crushed
2 tablespoons chopped fresh parsley
generous pinch of dried rosemary
salt and pepper

Mix the lamb with 1 tablespoon of the oil, the garlic, herbs
and seasoning. Form the mixture into 8 cakes using a 5 cm/2
inch pastry cutter to make neat shapes. Chill for 1 hour.

Brush the burgers with the remaining oil. Cook over a
preheated barbecue for about 15 minutes until golden brown,
turning occasionally.

96 BARBECUED FRENCH LEG OF LAMB

Preparation time:
15 minutes, plus
marinating

Cooking time:
1½-2 hours

Serves 6

Calories:
370 per portion

YOU WILL NEED:
2 tablespoons oil
2 tablespoons white wine
salt and pepper
1 × 1.5-2 kg/3-4 lb leg of lamb
2 garlic cloves, cut into thin slivers
fresh rosemary sprigs

Mix together the oil, wine and seasoning, and brush a little
over the leg of lamb. Make slits in the skin of the meat and insert the garlic slivers and rosemary sprigs. Put the lamb in a
large polythene bag with the remaining oil and wine mixture.
Marinate in the refrigerator for 2-4 hours, turning occasionally.

Insert a rotisserie spit carefully into the lamb. Cook over
a preheated barbecue for 1½-2 hours, brushing with the marinade occasionally. Put a few sprigs of rosemary on the fire for
extra flavour.

◼ COOK'S TIP

Look out for the specially
selected lean minced lamb
that is now available at
most major supermarkets.
Alternatively, remove all the
visible fat from a piece of
lamb such as fillet or
leg, and mince the meat
finely.

◼ COOK'S TIP

The taste of this lamb is
excellent, especially when it
is served slightly pink in the
centre. Rosemary is the herb
traditionally used with lamb
in France rather than mint.

97 SFERIA

Preparation time:
20 minutes, plus
marinating

Cooking time:
8-10 minutes

Serves 4

Calories:
535 per portion

YOU WILL NEED:
750 g/1½ lb minced lean lamb
finely grated rind of 1 orange
1 large garlic clove, crushed
1 teaspoon mixed spice
1 red pepper, cored, seeded and very
    finely chopped
25 g/1 oz raisins, chopped
salt and pepper
2 egg yolks
Apricot sauce (see Cook's Tip)
FOR THE MARINADE
5 tablespoons orange juice
6 tablespoons olive oil
2 tablespoons red wine

Mix the lamb with the orange rind, garlic, spice, red pepper, raisins and seasoning to taste. Work in the egg yolks. Divide the mixture into 20 portions and shape each into a ball. Put in a shallow dish.

Mix the marinade ingredients together and spoon over the meatballs. Marinate in the refrigerator, covered, for 4-6 hours, turning them once or twice.

Remove the meatballs from their marinade and drain, reserving the marinade. Thread the meatballs on to 4 kebab skewers. Brush with the marinade. Cook on the greased grill of a preheated barbecue for 8-10 minutes, turning them once and brushing with the remaining marinade. Serve with the hot sauce.

▮ COOK'S TIP

To make the sauce, fry 2 small finely chopped onions gently in 2 tablespoons olive oil for 2 minutes. Add 450 g/1 lb chopped fresh or drained canned apricots, 1 tablespoon chopped fresh mint, 150 ml/¼ pint dry white wine and 2 teaspoons clear honey. Simmer gently for 10 minutes.

98 WINCHESTER SAUSAGES

Preparation time:
30 minutes, plus
standing

Cooking time:
15-20 minutes

Makes about 12

Calories:
97 per sausage

YOU WILL NEED:
225 g/8 oz belly pork, minced
225 g/8 oz lean minced pork
25 g/1 oz pork fat, minced
6 tablespoons milk
75 g/3 oz wholemeal breadcrumbs
1 garlic clove, crushed
¼ teaspoon ground mace
¼ teaspoon allspice
1 tablespoon chopped parsley
1 tablespoon sage
1 teaspoon chopped thyme
salt and pepper
about 1 metre/3 ft sausage casing (see
    Cook's Tip)

Mix the pork and fat together in a bowl. Pour the milk over the breadcrumbs and leave for 10 minutes. Squeeze the breadcrumbs dry and add to the meat. Add the garlic, spices, herbs and seasoning to taste and mix well.

Using a piping bag fitted with a large plain nozzle, carefully force the sausage mixture into the casing. Push the mixture evenly along the casing, then twist to form sausages.

Cook on a barbecue grill, 10 cm/4 inches above the fire, for 15-20 minutes, until golden brown and thoroughly cooked.

▮ COOK'S TIP

Sausage casings are available from some butchers. They should be soaked overnight in cold water and drained before being used.

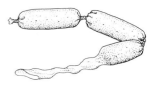

99 ORIENTAL SPARE RIBS

Preparation time:
15 minutes

Cooking time:
45-50 minutes

Serves 6

Calories:
414 per portion

YOU WILL NEED:
1 kg/2¼ lb pork spare ribs
FOR THE SAUCE
2 spring onions, chopped
2 garlic cloves, thinly sliced
2.5 cm/1 inch piece fresh root ginger,
    shredded
1 tablespoon soy sauce
4 tablespoons clear honey
3 tablespoons lemon juice
2 tablespoons mango chutney
½ teaspoon ground ginger
1 tablespoon oil
2 tablespoons dry sherry

Put the spare ribs on a greased grill 10 cm/4 inches above a preheated barbecue.

Put all the sauce ingredients in a pan over a low heat, gradually bring to the boil and cook for 1 minute.

Spoon the sauce over the ribs, covering them all well. Return to the barbecue and cook for 15-20 minutes, basting the spare ribs frequently.

Serve hot or cold.

100 UCCELLETTI DI CAMPAGNA SENZA TESTA

Preparation time:
30 minutes, plus
standing

Cooking time:
6-8 minutes

Serves 4

Calories:
387 per portion

YOU WILL NEED:
50 g/2 oz sultanas
4 tablespoons Marsala
4 long thin pork escalopes, about
    75 g/3 oz each
4 thin slices Parma ham
1 tablespoon chopped fresh sage
salt and pepper
16 cubes white bread, about 2.5 cm/
    1 inch square
4 tablespoons olive oil
8 thin rashers rindless streaky bacon,
    halved crossways

Mix the sultanas with the Marsala; cover and leave to stand for 1 hour.

Cut each pork escalope into 4 long strips; cut the slices of ham into strips roughly the same size. Lay a strip of ham on top of each strip of pork. Sprinkle each strip with some sage, a few sultanas and seasoning to taste, then roll each strip up neatly, to make 16 sausage shapes.

Brush each cube of bread with olive oil, then roll in half a rasher of streaky bacon.

Thread 4 pork and ham rolls and 4 bread and bacon rolls alternately on to each of 4 kebab skewers; brush the skewers with olive oil. Cook on the greased grill of a preheated barbecue for 3-4 minutes on each side. Serve hot.

■ COOK'S TIP

If the pieces of mango in the chutney are large, chop them coarsely before adding to the other ingredients for the sauce.

■ COOK'S TIP

Try using ciabatta or other Italian bread to give a distinctive taste to the cubes. As Parma ham is expensive, other air-dried ham can be substituted.

101 CITRUS CHICKEN

Preparation time:
15 minutes, plus
marinating

Cooking time:
20 minutes

Serves 4

Calories:
243 per portion

YOU WILL NEED:

1 garlic clove, crushed
3 tablespoons lemon juice
4 tablespoons orange juice
salt and pepper
pinch of ground cinnamon
4 chicken joints, skinned
oil

Mix the garlic with the lemon and orange juice, add seasoning
and the cinnamon. Pour into a shallow dish and add the
chicken. Marinate for 4 hours.

Drain the chicken, reserving any marinade, and brush
with oil. Cook on a greased grill over a preheated barbecue
for about 10 minutes on each side. If any marinade is left, it
can be heated and poured over the chicken before serving.

102 CURRIED CHICKEN KEBABS

Preparation time:
35 minutes, plus
standing

Cooking time:
13 minutes

Serves 4

Calories:
352 per portion

YOU WILL NEED:

12 tiny onions or shallots
50 g/2 oz butter
2 teaspoons mild curry powder
squeeze of lemon juice
salt and pepper
4 small chicken breasts, skinned,
*   boned and cut into 2.5 cm/1 inch*
*   cubes*
4 chicken livers, trimmed and halved
8 button mushrooms
1 green pepper, cored, seeded and
*   diced*

Simmer the onions or shallots in a very little water for 3
minutes. Drain. Melt the butter and blend with the curry
powder, lemon juice and seasoning. Add the chicken cubes
and leave for 10 minutes.

Thread the chicken, chicken livers, mushrooms and green
pepper alternately on to 4 skewers. Brush the liver and vegetables with any remaining curried butter. Cook over a preheated barbecue for about 10 minutes, turning several times.

■ COOK'S TIP

Insert the tip of a small,
sharp, pointed knife under
the skin of the chicken
joints and loosen a small
piece. The skin can then be
pulled off quite easily.

■ COOK'S TIP

A small, sharp, pointed
knife is essential for boning
the chicken breasts. Scrape
the flesh away from the
bones carefully. Use the
bones to make stock.

103 BARBECUED BEEF ROLLS

Preparation time:
10 minutes, plus
marinating

Cooking time:
15-20 minutes

Serves 4

Calories:
377 per portion

YOU WILL NEED:
8 small onions
4 minute steaks
4 small mushrooms
Oriental marinade (see Cook's Tip)

Blanch the onions in boiling water for 2-3 minutes. Drain well.

Flatten the steaks with a cutlet bat or rolling pin. Place 2 onions and a mushroom in the centre of each steak and roll the meat around the vegetables. Secure with a skewer. Place the steak rolls in a shallow dish and pour over the marinade. Marinate in the refrigerator for 2-3 hours.

Cook over a preheated barbecue for 10-15 minutes, turning frequently and brushing with the marinade.

104 CURRY BURGERS

Preparation time:
25 minutes, plus
chilling

Cooking time:
20-22 minutes

Serves 10

Calories:
415 per portion

YOU WILL NEED:
450 g/1 lb minced bacon
1 kg/2¼ lb minced beef
4 tablespoons chopped parsley
1 large onion, grated
2 teaspoons curry powder
1 garlic clove, crushed
6 spring onions, finely chopped
2 eggs, beaten
salt and pepper
oil
10 slices cheese each about 5 mm/
¼ inch thick
10 tablespoons chutney

Mix all the ingredients together, except the oil, cheese and chutney, until blended. Chill for 30 minutes.

Mould the mixture into 10 neat burger shapes and brush with oil. Seal quickly on both sides, on the grill over a preheated barbecue.

Cut out 10 squares of foil, each about 23 cm/9 inches square. Place a burger in the centre of each foil square and top with a slice of cheese and a spoonful of chutney. Pinch the edges of the foil up and over the burgers and pleat together. Cook the burgers over the fire for about 20 minutes.

■ COOK'S TIP

For the Oriental marinade combine 4 tablespoons soy sauce, 2 tablespoons clear honey, 4 tablespoons sherry, 1 teaspoon ground cinnamon, ½ teaspoon ground cloves, 4 tablespoons cold tea, 1 crushed garlic clove and pepper to taste.

■ COOK'S TIP

Choose a cheese that melts well and does not become stringy. As the burgers are strongly seasoned, a bland-tasting cheese is suitable.

105 PICADILLO ANDALUZIA

Preparation time:
25 minutes, plus chilling

Cooking time:
17-20 minutes

Serves 6

Calories:
582 per portion

YOU WILL NEED:

1 kg/2¼ lb minced beef
1 onion, finely chopped
1 garlic clove, crushed
¼ teaspoon chilli powder
salt and pepper
30 blanched almonds
oil, for brushing
Pepper, olive and nut sauce (see Cook's Tip)

Mix together the minced beef with the onion, garlic, chilli powder and seasoning to taste. Divide the mixture into 30 equal portions and shape each one into a ball; press a whole almond into the centre. Chill for 4 hours.

Thread 5 meatballs on to each of 6 skewers. Brush on all sides with oil. Cook the meatballs on the greased grill of a preheated barbecue for 8-10 minutes, turning once.

Serve with the hot Pepper, olive and nut sauce.

106 KOUAH

Preparation time:
25 minutes, plus chilling

Cooking time:
6-8 minutes

Serves 4

Calories:
473 per portion

YOU WILL NEED:

750 g/1½ lb calf's liver, preferably in one thick piece
24 thin rashers rindless streaky bacon
8 tablespoons olive oil
2 teaspoons ground cumin
2 teaspoons paprika pepper
½ teaspoon cayenne
salt
4 tablespoons white wine vinegar

Cut the liver into 24 equal pieces; roll each piece in a bacon rasher and secure with a cocktail stick. Put the liver rolls in a shallow dish. Mix the olive oil with the cumin, paprika, cayenne and salt to taste. Spoon evenly over the liver rolls, cover and chill for at least 4 hours, turning them once.

Remove the liver rolls from the marinade and drain, reserving the marinade. Remove the cocktail sticks and thread 6 rolls on to each of 4 kebab skewers. Brush the kebabs with a little of the marinade.

Cook on the greased grill of a preheated barbecue for 3-4 minutes on each side. Remove the kebabs from the grill, sprinkle with the vinegar and serve immediately.

■ COOK'S TIP

For the sauce, fry 1 chopped onion briefly in 2 tablespoons oil. Add 450 g/1 lb chopped tomatoes, 2 tablespoons tomato purée, 1 grated apple, 450 ml/¾ pint red wine, 2 small chopped red chillies, 25 g/1 oz raisins and seasoning. Cook 6-7 minutes. Stir in sliced stuffed olives and chopped almonds to taste.

■ COOK'S TIP

If calf's liver seems extravagant, use lamb's liver instead. It should be marinated in the flavoured oil for 6-8 hours and will take slightly longer to cook.

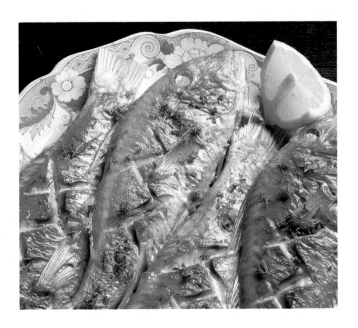

107 RED MULLET WITH FENNEL

Preparation time:
20 minutes

Cooking time:
20-30 minutes

Serves 4

Calories:
643 per portion

YOU WILL NEED:
4 red mullet, scaled, cleaned and
     washed
6-8 fennel sprigs
olive oil
juice of 1 lemon
lemon wedges

Score the fish lightly on each side with a sharp knife. Reserve 2 tablespoons of chopped fennel leaves. Chop up the remaining leaves finely with the stalks. Lay the fish on a double thickness of foil and stuff them with some of the fennel, laying the rest of it between the fish. Sprinkle with olive oil and some of the lemon juice. Cook over a preheated barbecue for about 20-30 minutes, brushing the fish with oil and lemon juice occasionally.

Sprinkle the red mullet with the reserved fennel and serve with lemon wedges.

108 TRIGLIA ALLA CALABRESE

Preparation time:
30 minutes

Cooking time:
20 minutes

Serves 6

Calories:
413 per portion

YOU WILL NEED:
6 red mullet, about 225 g/8 oz each,
     scaled, cleaned and washed
salt and pepper
2 tablespoons chopped fresh oregano
     or 2 teaspoons dried oregano
2 tablespoons chopped parsley
75 g/3 oz stoned black olives, sliced
2 tablespoons capers
4 tablespoons olive oil
1 garlic clove, crushed

Sprinkle the red mullet inside and out with salt and pepper. Fill the cavities of the fish with half of the oregano and parsley. Place each fish on a rectangle of oiled foil and pull up the sides.

Mix the remaining oregano and parsley with the olives, capers, olive oil and garlic. Spoon the mixture evenly over the fish. Cover each fish with foil, pinching the edges together well to seal.

Cook on the greased grill of a preheated barbecue until the fish is tender – about 20 minutes. Serve with jacket potatoes.

■ COOK'S TIP

*If you are unfamiliar with
preparing red mullet, ask
your fishmonger to show
you how to scale and clean
the fish. Lemon juice brings
out the delicate flavour.*

■ COOK'S TIP

*For crisp-skinned red
mullet, fill the cavity of each
fish with the oregano,
parsley, olives, capers and
garlic, brush with oil and
cook over a barbecue.*

109 TLETAS

Preparation time:
15 minutes

Cooking time:
5 minutes

Serves 4

Calories:
882 per portion

YOU WILL NEED:
16 medium sardines
1 tablespoon ground cumin
3 garlic cloves, crushed
1 teaspoon cayenne
pinch of salt
wedges of lemon or lime, to serve

Split each sardine down its belly; clean the fish if preferred.

Mix the cumin, garlic, cayenne and salt together. Rub the mixture well into the sardines.

Fit the fish into a fish clamp or sardine grill and cook over the greased grill of a preheated barbecue for about 5 minutes. Serve piping hot with wedges of lemon or lime and a cucumber and yogurt salad.

110 CREVETTES GRILLEES AU BEURRE BASILIC

Preparation time:
30 minutes

Cooking time:
4 minutes

Serves 6

Calories:
280 per portion

YOU WILL NEED:
24 large uncooked Mediterranean
  prawns
salt and pepper
olive oil
175 g/6 oz butter
24 large fresh basil leaves, roughly
  chopped
2 large garlic cloves, crushed
1-2 sprigs fresh basil, to garnish

Split each prawn by cutting carefully along the belly and through the head and tail, but leaving the back shell intact. Open out each prawn so that it lies flat. Season the cut surfaces with salt and pepper and brush both sides generously with olive oil.

Cook on the greased grill of a preheated barbecue, shell side downwards, for 2 minutes. Turn the prawns over and cook for a further 2 minutes.

Meanwhile melt the butter in a small pan and add the chopped basil and garlic – this can be done on the side of the barbecue.

Arrange the grilled prawns, flesh side uppermost, on a flat serving dish. Spoon the hot basil butter over and garnish with the sprigs of fresh basil.

Serve immediately with a green salad and warm crusty bread to mop up the basil butter.

▨ COOK'S TIP

If you do not have a fish clamp or sardine grill, cook the sardines on a double layer of foil placed shiny side uppermost on top of the barbecue grill.

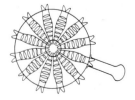

▨ COOK'S TIP

Many supermarkets now sell packets of fresh basil in the greengrocery section. It can be easily grown at home in a pot on a sunny windowsill.

111 SEAFOOD KEBABS

Preparation time:
40 minutes, plus
marinating

Cooking time:
10-14 minutes

Serves 8

Calories:
295 per portion

YOU WILL NEED:
225 g/8 oz plaice fillets
4 sardines or other small fish
8 large cooked unshelled prawns
4 scallops, halved
8 rashers rindless streaky bacon
bay leaves
lemon wedges
FOR THE MARINADE
juice of 1 lemon
4 tablespoons olive oil
1 bouquet garni
salt and pepper
FOR THE SAUCE
6 tablespoons mayonnaise
1 garlic clove, crushed
1 teaspoon tomato purée
dash of Tabasco sauce
1 tablespoon each chopped parsley,
    thyme and capers

Cut the plaice into chunks and the sardines into halves. Mix the marinade ingredients add all the fish and mix well. Leave to marinate for 30 minutes, stirring occasionally.

Mix the sauce ingredients together.

Drain the marinade from the fish and reserve. Cut the bacon rashers in half and roll up. Arrange the fish, bacon, bay leaves and lemon wedges on skewers. Cook 10 cm/4 inches above a preheated barbecue, for 5-7 minutes on each side, basting with the marinade. Serve hot, with the cold sauce.

▓ COOK'S TIP

Packets of dried bouquet garni are widely available. If preferred, wrap a selection of fresh herbs including a bay leaf in a piece of muslin.

112 SPICY FRUIT KEBABS

Preparation time:
15 minutes

Cooking time:
8-10 minutes

Serves 8

Calories:
178 per portion

YOU WILL NEED:
2 oranges
2 red-skinned apples
2 bananas
16 pineapple chunks, fresh or canned
100 g/4 oz butter
2 tablespoons soft light brown sugar
1 teaspoon ground allspice or
    coriander

Cut each orange into 4 thick slices and halve each slice. Core the apples and cut each into 4 wedges. Cut each banana into 4 thick slices. Thread 2 orange pieces, 1 apple wedge, 1 banana slice and 2 pineapple chunks on to each of 8 skewers.

Melt the butter in a saucepan over a preheated barbecue on the side of the fire. Stir in the sugar and spice.

Place the fruit kebabs on the barbecue grid, about 15 cm/6 inches above the fire. Brush with the spice butter and cook for about 5 minutes, basting frequently and turning to brown on all sides.

▓ COOK'S TIP

If it is necessary to prepare the fruit in advance, remember to brush the apples and bananas thoroughly with lemon juice to prevent discoloration.

These kebabs are ideal for vegetarian guests at a barbecue party.

113 LA PETITE SALADE DE CAILLE ET JAMBON

Preparation time:
30 minutes

Cooking time:
20 minutes

Oven temperature:
190 C, 375 F, gas 5

Serves 8

Calories:
311 per portion

YOU WILL NEED:

8 quail, plucked and cleaned
salt and pepper
about 150 ml/¼ pint walnut or olive
    oil
½ a medium head curly endive
8 canned artichoke hearts, well
    drained and quartered
4 thin slices Parma ham, cut into
    strips
100 g/4 oz pâté de foie, chilled
1 garlic clove, crushed
1 tablespoon chopped fresh tarragon
3 tablespoons orange juice

Put the quail into a small roasting tin; season with salt and pepper and spoon 4 tablespoons of the oil over. Cover with foil and cook in a preheated oven for 20 minutes – the quail should still be slightly pink.

Strip the leaves off the endive, discarding any that are wilted; wash and shake dry. Arrange the leaves on a large, flat dish. Cut the pâté into 4 slices. Arrange the artichokes, strips of ham and slices of pâté around the edge of the dish.

Mix the remaining walnut oil with the garlic, tarragon, orange juice and seasoning to taste.

Halve the cooked quail; discard any splintered pieces of bone. Arrange the quail halves, cut surface downwards, in the centre of the salad. Spoon the prepared dressing over the quail and salad and serve immediately.

■ COOK'S TIP

Cook the quail over a barbecue if preferred – wrap each bird in thin rindless rashers of bacon and thread on to skewers. Cook for 10-12 minutes.

114 COURGETTES A LA GRECQUE

Preparation time:
20 minutes, plus
draining and
chilling

Cooking time:
25-30 minutes

Serves 4

Calories:
350 per portion

YOU WILL NEED:

450 g/1 lb courgettes, topped and
    tailed
1½ tablespoons salt
150 ml/¼ pint olive oil
150 ml/¼ pint water
1 bay leaf
1 tablespoon chopped fresh thyme
1 teaspoon coriander seeds, crushed
½ teaspoon black peppercorns,
    crushed
1 tablespoon lemon juice
4 large tomatoes, skinned, seeded and
    chopped
1 large garlic clove, finely chopped

Cut each courgette into lengthways slices about 5 mm/¼ inch thick. Put the slices into a colander and sprinkle with the salt; leave to drain for 1 hour. Rinse the courgette slices and pat them dry on absorbent kitchen paper.

Put the remaining ingredients into a deep frying pan. Bring to the boil and simmer for 5 minutes. Add the courgette slices to the pan. Cover and simmer gently for about 20 minutes.

Transfer to a shallow serving dish; allow to cool, cover and then chill for at least 2 hours before serving.

■ COOK'S TIP

Serve the courgettes as a starter with plenty of hot crusty bread, or as an accompaniment to barbecued meat or fish. The courgettes can be prepared up to 24 hours in advance, covered and chilled until they are required.

115 SALADE DE PISSENLITS

Preparation time:
10 minutes

Cooking time:
5 minutes

Serves 4

Calories:
114 per portion

YOU WILL NEED:
350 g/12 oz dandelion leaves or mâche
  (see Cook's Tip)
2 tablespoons olive oil
75 g/3 oz rindless streaky bacon,
  chopped
2 tablespoons white wine vinegar
salt and pepper

Wash the leaves, tear them into pieces and put in a bowl.

Heat the olive oil in a frying pan. Add the chopped bacon and fry gently until the bacon fat runs. Add the wine vinegar and seasoning to taste and heat until the vinegar bubbles; spoon immediately over the dandelion leaves and toss well.

Serve immediately.

116 BARBECUED CORN ON THE COB

Preparation time:
5 minutes

Cooking time:
1 hour 10 minutes

Serves 4

Calories:
326 per portion

YOU WILL NEED:
4 fresh corn-on-the-cob
100 g/4 oz butter
1 tablespoon finely chopped parsley
salt and pepper

Fold back the husks from the corn and remove the silky hairs. Cut out the cob but retain the husk. Blanch the corn in boiling water for 7 minutes. Drain and replace in the husks. Cook over a preheated barbecue on the side of the fire for about 1 hour or until tender.

Mix the butter, parsley and seasoning together to serve with the hot corn.

■ COOK'S TIP

Dandelion leaves and mâche can be bought in shops that specialize in unusual vegetables; or wild dandelion leaves can be used.

■ COOK'S TIP

If preferred, cook the corn with the parsley butter in foil parcels. Make sure the parcels are sealed tightly enough to prevent the butter from seeping out as this *would cause flames on the barbecue. Cook for 20-25 minutes or until the corn is tender.*

117 PEPPER, ANCHOVY AND TOMATO SALAD

Preparation time:
20 minutes, plus chilling

Cooking time:
about 5 minutes

Serves 4

Calories:
158 per portion

YOU WILL NEED:
2 large red peppers
3 large tomatoes, skinned, sliced and seeded (see Cook's Tip)
2 × 50 g/2 oz cans anchovy fillets, drained
4 tablespoons olive oil
2 tablespoons lemon juice
1 garlic clove, crushed
salt and pepper

Place the peppers under a preheated hot grill, and cook, turning them frequently, until the skins are charred. Remove from the grill and place under cold running water. Remove the cores and seeds and cut the flesh into wide strips.

Arrange the peppers on a flat serving dish with the sliced tomatoes. Rinse the anchovy fillets under cold running water and lay a lattice of anchovy fillets on top of the peppers and tomatoes. Mix together the oil, lemon juice, garlic and seasoning. Pour over the salad and chill for 30 minutes before serving.

118 POTATO SALAD

Preparation time:
20 minutes plus chilling

Serves 4

Calories:
342 per portion

YOU WILL NEED:
450 g/1 lb waxy potatoes, cooked, peeled and sliced (see Cook's Tip)
120 ml/4 fl oz mayonnaise
1 tablespoon lemon juice
1 tablespoon olive or good vegetable oil
salt and pepper
2 tablespoons finely chopped fresh chives
4 tablespoons finely chopped leeks

Place the potatoes in a mixing bowl. Mix together the mayonnaise, lemon juice, oil, seasoning and 1 tablespoon of the chives. Add the mixture to the potato slices and toss gently until well coated.

Spoon the mixture into a serving bowl. Sprinkle with the remaining chives and scatter the leeks around the edge of the bowl.

Cover and chill in the refrigerator for 30 minutes before serving.

■ COOK'S TIP

Choose firm but ripe tomatoes for this salad and use a serrated knife to slice them neatly. Remove the seeds and white core from each slice with a teaspoon.

■ COOK'S TIP

If the potatoes are small and new, try rubbing the skins off with your fingers rather than using a knife or potato peeler. This way no potato is wasted.

119 RED SALAD

Preparation time:
20 minutes, plus
standing

Serves 6

Calories:
95 per portion

YOU WILL NEED:
4 tablespoons olive or good vegetable
  oil
3 garlic cloves, crushed
salt and pepper
1 tablespoon red wine vinegar
225 g/8 oz red cabbage, finely
  shredded
1 head of radicchio
2 red-skinned apples
1 small red onion
1 bunch of radishes
2 tomatoes

Combine the oil, garlic and salt and pepper to taste. Add the
red wine vinegar.

Place the cabbage in a bowl with the dressing. Toss well
and leave for 1 hour.

Separate the radicchio into leaves, then tear into pieces;
thinly slice the apples, onion and radishes; cut the tomatoes in
half, then in pieces. Add to the bowl and toss thoroughly,
then transfer to a salad bowl.

120 CUCUMBER WITH MINT

Preparation time:
15 minutes, plus
standing

Serves 4

Calories:
30 per portion

YOU WILL NEED:
1 cucumber, thinly sliced
salt and pepper
1 bunch of mint, finely chopped
FOR THE DRESSING
150 ml/¼ pint natural yogurt
1 garlic clove, crushed
1 tablespoon cider vinegar
1 teaspoon clear honey

Place the cucumber in a colander, sprinkle with salt and leave
to drain for 30 minutes.

Meanwhile prepare the dressing. Place all the ingredients
in a bowl and add salt and pepper to taste. Mix thoroughly
with a fork.

Dry the cucumber on absorbent kitchen paper and place
in a shallow serving dish. Add the mint and dressing and mix
well.

■ COOK'S TIP

*If a less strongly flavoured
dressing is preferred, place a
garlic clove in a small bottle
of oil and leave for 2-3 days
before using in the dressing
in place of the oil and three*
*garlic cloves. Remember to
label the bottle so the garlic
oil is not used inadvertently!*

■ COOK'S TIP

*This is a very refreshing and
popular salad to serve with
strongly seasoned barbecue
fare. It is also a delicious
accompaniment to plain
grilled white fish.*

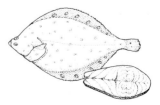

121 SEAFOOD SAUCE

Preparation time:
10 minutes

Makes about
150 ml/¼ pint

Toal calories: 1,044

YOU WILL NEED:
150 ml/¼ pint mayonnaise
1 tablespoon tomato purée
1 teaspoon grated lemon rind
2 tablespoons lemon juice
1 teaspoon Worcestershire sauce
few drops of Tabasco sauce
1 teaspoon finely grated onion or
spring onion
1 tablespoon chopped fresh parsley
salt and pepper

Put the ingredients in a bowl and stir thoroughly to combine.
Add salt and pepper to taste.

122 CREOLE SAUCE

Preparation time:
10 minutes

Cooking time:
25-30 minutes

Makes about
150 ml/¼ pint

Total calories: 396

YOU WILL NEED:
2 tablespoons oil
1 large onion, finely chopped
1 green pepper, cored, seeded and
finely chopped
1 × 400 g/14 oz can tomatoes
1 small can red pimientos, drained and
chopped
1 teaspoon caster sugar
generous pinch of dry mustard
pinch of chilli powder (optional)
1 tablespoon lemon juice
salt and pepper
1 tablespoon chopped parsley

Heat the oil in a saucepan and fry the onion and green pepper
until soft. Add the tomatoes, with the can juice, the pimientos, sugar, mustard, chilli powder, if using, lemon juice and
seasoning. Stir well and bring to the boil. Simmer for 20
minutes. Stir in the chopped parsley before serving.

■ COOK'S TIP

For special occasions, add
2-3 tablespoons lightly
whipped cream to the sauce
just before serving. Fold in
gently. Ideally, use home-
made mayonnaise.

■ COOK'S TIP

This sauce may be served
hot or cold. When having a
barbecue party, make a
large batch (double the
recipe quantities) so that
your guests can help

themselves. It can also be
used to brush meat while it
is being cooked over a
barbecue.

123 SPICY HORSERADISH SAUCE

Preparation time:
5 minutes, plus
chilling

Makes about
150 ml/¼ pint

Total calories: 652

YOU WILL NEED:
150 ml/¼ pint double cream
1 tablespoon lemon juice
2 teaspoons peeled and grated
  horseradish
2 teaspoons Worcestershire sauce
2 spring onions, finely chopped

Whip the cream lightly. Stir in the lemon juice, horseradish,
Worcestershire sauce and spring onions. Chill for 4 hours
before serving.

124 PINEAPPLE AND CIDER SAUCE

Preparation time:
5 minutes

Cooking time:
5 minutes

Makes about
300 ml/½ pint

Total calories: 258

YOU WILL NEED:
1 tablespoon cornflour
300 ml/½ pint dry cider
100 g/4 oz pineapple, chopped
25 g/1 oz seedless raisins

Dissolve the cornflour in a little of the cider. Heat the remaining cider in a saucepan, then stir into the cornflour. Return to
the pan and bring to the boil, stirring. Add the pineapple and
raisins and heat through.

■ COOK'S TIP

Horseradish is a traditional
accompaniment of roast
beef so serve this tasty sauce
with barbecued beef dishes.

■ COOK'S TIP

This sauce is particularly
delicious served with dishes
containing pork, bacon or
ham. Either fresh or drained
canned pineapple (in natural
juice rather than sweetened

syrup) can be used
depending on availability
and personal preference.

125 ICED LEMON RICE PUDDING

Preparation time:
20 minutes, plus
standing and
chilling

Cooking time:
25-30 minutes

Serves 6

Calories:
164 per portion

YOU WILL NEED:
thinly pared rind of 1 lemon
600 ml/1 pint milk
50 g/2 oz caster sugar
100 g/4 oz Italian round-grain or
  pudding rice
finely grated rind of 1 lemon
2 eggs
thinly pared lemon rind, to decorate

Put the pared lemon rind into a pan with the milk; bring just to the boil and leave to infuse for 30 minutes.

Strain the milk into a clean pan and stir in the sugar. Stir in the rice and cook gently until the rice is tender but still slightly firm and all the milk has been absorbed, about 25 minutes. Turn the rice into a bowl and beat in the grated lemon rind and the eggs. Turn into a greased 900 ml/1½ pint mould. Chill for 4-6 hours.

Carefully turn out the set rice on to a serving dish. Decorate with strips of lemon rind.

126 MARMALADE ICE CREAM

Preparation time:
25 minutes, plus
freezing

Cooking time:
7-9 minutes

Serves 6

Calories:
236 per portion

YOU WILL NEED:
100 g/4 oz caster sugar
250 ml/8 fl oz water
1 tablespoon lemon juice
4 tablespoons orange marmalade
300 ml/½ pint natural yogurt
150 ml/¼ pint double or whipping
  cream

Put the sugar, water and lemon juice in a heavy-based saucepan and heat gently until the sugar has dissolved. Increase the heat and cook rapidly until the syrup reaches 140 C/280 F on a sugar thermometer.

Stir in the marmalade and allow the mixture to become cold. Stir in the yogurt. Pour the mixture into a freezer container and freeze for about 1½ hours or until very mushy.

Beat the cream until it forms soft peaks. Fold into the yogurt mixture and freeze for 2 hours, beating the mixture at hourly intervals. Cover, seal and freeze until firm.

■ COOK'S TIP

Serve the small Italian
macaroons known as
Amaretti with this pudding.
The almond flavour
combines beautifully with
the lemon.

■ COOK'S TIP

To make a more piquant ice
cream, add 1 teaspoon
chopped stem ginger to the
recipe, adding it with the
marmalade, or use ginger
marmalade instead.

127 SUMMER PUDDING

Preparation time:
25 minutes, plus
chilling

Cooking time:
about 20 minutes

Serves 6

Calories:
288 per portion

YOU WILL NEED:
6-8 slices white bread, crusts removed
1 × 575 g/1¼ lb can rhubarb
250 g/9 oz blackcurrants
250 g/9 oz cooking apples, peeled,
*   cored and sliced*
175 g/6 oz caster sugar
100 g/4 oz raspberries or strawberries

Put one slice of bread aside for the top and use the remainder to line the bottom and sides of a 900 ml/1½ pint pudding basin, fitting the slices closely together. Drain the rhubarb, reserving 4 tablespoons of the can juice. Put the juice in a pan with the blackcurrants, apples and sugar and cook gently until tender but not too mushy, stirring occasionally. Add the raspberries or strawberries and continue cooking for 2 minutes. Spoon all the fruit into the bread-lined basin, reserving a little of the juice, and cover with the last piece of bread. Fold the edges of the bread over the slice on top. Spoon the reserved juice down the sides of the basin. Cover with a saucer and a weight or heavy can. Leave to cool, then chill overnight in the refrigerator.

Turn out the pudding carefully just before serving.

128 GRAPEFRUIT AND MINT ICE CREAM

Preparation time:
25 minutes, plus
freezing

Cooking time:
7-9 minutes

Serves 6

Calories:
215 per portion

YOU WILL NEED:
2 grapefruit
100 g/4 oz caster sugar
175 ml/6 oz water
300 ml/½ pint natural yogurt
1 tablespoon chopped fresh mint
150 ml/¼ pint double or whipping
*   cream*

Cut the skin and pith from the grapefruit. Separate the segments, cutting them away from the membranes. Chop the segments finely, reserving any juice.

Put the sugar and water in a heavy-based saucepan and heat gently until the sugar has dissolved. Increase the heat and cook rapidly until the syrup reaches 140 C/280 F on a sugar thermometer. Allow to cool.

Stir the chopped grapefruit, yogurt and mint into the syrup. Pour into a freezer container and freeze for about 1½ hours until mushy.

Beat the cream until it forms soft peaks. Fold into the mixture and freeze for 2 hours, beating the mixture at hourly intervals. Cover, seal and freeze until firm.

■ COOK'S TIP

Depending on availability, other fruits such as damsons and redcurrants and even gooseberries can be used instead of the blackcurrants. Remember to remove any *stones before spooning the fruit mixture into the bread-lined basin.*

■ COOK'S TIP

The best type of sugar thermometer to use is one that clips on to the side of the saucepan. As it stays in an upright position, the reading will be accurate.

SPECIAL OCCASIONS

Parties given to celebrate special occasions should be memorable, so indulge in some luxurious dishes. This chapter includes festive recipes for Christmas and Easter as well as suggestions for both a Mediterranean-style and an Indian party. Other recipes are perfect for family celebrations like christenings and birthdays.

129 TRADITIONAL ROAST BEEF

Preparation time:
15-20 minutes

Cooking time:
2-2½ hours

Oven temperature:
220 C, 425 F, gas 7

Serves 8

Calories:
811 per portion

YOU WILL NEED:
1.75-2.25 kg/4-5 lb boned and rolled
 sirloin rib
salt and pepper
50 g/2 oz dripping
FOR THE YORKSHIRE PUDDINGS
100 g/4 oz plain flour
2 eggs
300 ml/½ pint milk
a little dripping

Place the joint in a roasting tin with the thickest layer of fat uppermost. Season lightly with salt and pepper and spread with the dripping. Roast in a preheated oven, basting several times, for the calculated time (see Cook's Tip). Roast potatoes alongside the joint for the last 1½ hours of cooking.

Meanwhile make the Yorkshire puddings: sift the flour with a pinch of salt into a mixing bowl and make a well in the centre. Add the eggs and gradually beat in the milk to give a smooth batter. Add a little dripping to 8 Yorkshire pudding tins or 16-18 patty tins and heat in the oven until piping hot. Pour the batter into the tins and bake below the joint for the last 25 minutes of cooking or until well puffed up and brown.

Transfer the joint to a warmed serving dish and surround with the roast potatoes and Yorkshire puddings.

130 TRADITIONAL ENGLISH ROAST TURKEY

Preparation time:
30 minutes

Cooking time:
3¾-4 hours

Oven temperature:
160 C, 325 F, gas 3

Serves 10

Calories:
869 per portion

YOU WILL NEED:
1 turkey (4.5-5.5 kg/10-12 lb)
chosen stuffings
50 g/2 oz butter, melted
salt and pepper
giblet stock (see Cook's Tip)
2 tablespoons flour
hot stuffing balls, to garnish

Wash the turkey and dry thoroughly. Spoon the stuffings into the bird. Sew both openings with trussing string, securing with skewers. Brush the turkey with the butter and sprinkle with salt and pepper. Cover with greased greaseproof paper or foil and place on a rack in a roasting tin. Roast in a preheated oven for 3¾-4 hours, basting and turning occasionally. Remove the paper or foil for the last 15 minutes.

Transfer the turkey to a hot serving platter. Discard the paper or foil, trussing string, and skewers (if used). Arrange hot stuffing balls around the bird. Keep hot. Drain off the surplus fat from the roasting tin, leaving the sediment. Place the tin on top of the stove and stir in the flour. Cook for 1-2 minutes, stirring constantly, then gradually add the giblet stock. Bring to the boil, stirring constantly, then lower the heat and simmer gently for 1-2 minutes. Adjust seasoning.

■ COOK'S TIP

Cooking times per 450 g/1 lb: rare – 20 minutes, plus 20 minutes extra; medium – 25 minutes, plus 25 minutes; well-done – 30 minutes, plus 30 minutes.

■ COOK'S TIP

For giblet stock, put the gizzard, heart and liver in a saucepan and cover with water. Add a sliced carrot, a slice of onion, a bay leaf, and salt and pepper. Bring to the *boil, then simmer gently for about 1 hour. Strain. Make up to 600 ml/1 pint with vegetable cooking water.*

131 CHOCOLATE CHESTNUT CHARLOTTE

Preparation time:
25-30 minutes, plus
chilling

Serves 8

Calories:
635 per portion

YOU WILL NEED:
100 g/4 oz plain chocolate, chopped
300 ml/½ pint milk
2 eggs, separated
50 g/2 oz soft light brown sugar
15 g/½ oz powdered gelatine
1 × 225 g/8 oz can unsweetened
   chestnut purée
300 ml/½ pint double cream, whipped
30 Langue de Chat biscuits
chocolate triangles (see Cook's Tip)

Heat the chocolate in a small pan with the milk over a low heat until melted. Beat the egg yolks and sugar until creamy, then stir in the chocolate. Return to the pan and heat gently, stirring until thickened. Dissolve the gelatine in 3 tablespoons hot water over a pan of simmering water; then stir into the chocolate custard. Beat the chestnut purée with a little of the chocolate custard until smooth, then mix in the remainder. Cool, then fold in two-thirds of the cream. Whisk the egg whites until stiff and fold in. Turn into a lightly oiled deep 18 cm/1 inch cake tin and chill until set.

   Turn out on to a plate and cover with a thin layer of whipped cream. Press the biscuits around the side; trim to fit if necessary. Decorate with the remaining cream and the chocolate triangles.

■ COOK'S TIP

To make the chocolate triangles, spread some melted chocolate thinly on greaseproof paper. When the chocolate has just set, cut into triangles with a small sharp knife. If necessary, make a greaseproof paper pattern of a triangle to ensure each one is the same size.

132 CHRISTMAS PUDDINGS

Preparation time:
about 30 minutes

Cooking time:
6-8 hours, plus 3-4
hours before serving

**Makes 1 large and 1
small pudding**

Calories:
3,589 per large
pudding
1,795 per small
pudding

YOU WILL NEED:
100 g/4 oz self-raising flour
175 g/6 oz fresh white breadcrumbs
175 g/6 oz currants
175 g/6 oz sultanas
100 g/4 oz stoned dates, chopped
225 g/8 oz stoned raisins
175 g/6 oz shredded suet
50 g/2 oz cut mixed peel
50 g/2 oz blanched almonds, chopped
1 small apple, peeled, cored and
   grated
grated rind and juice of 1 small orange
½ teaspoon mixed spice
¼ teaspoon ground or grated nutmeg
½ teaspoon salt
3 eggs
4 tablespoons brown ale or cider
225 g/8 oz dark soft brown sugar
oil for greasing basins

Thoroughly combine all the ingredients in a large mixing bowl. Turn into a well-greased 1.15 litre/2 pint and a 600 ml/1 pint basin and cover with greased greaseproof paper and foil. Tie securely with string.

   Boil or steam for 6-8 hours, depending on size. Top up the pan with more boiling water as necessary. Leave to cool overnight, then remove the coverings and cover again with fresh greased greaseproof paper and foil. Store in a cool dry place. Boil or steam for 3-4 hours before serving.

■ COOK'S TIP

If you have a pressure cooker, use this to cook the puddings in about half the time needed otherwise. Follow the manufacturer's instructions carefully.

133 CHOCOLATE LOG

Preparation time:
40 minutes

Cooking time:
8-10 minutes

Oven temperature:
200 C, 400 F, gas 6

Makes 1

Calories:
2,976 per whole
cake

YOU WILL NEED:
3 large eggs
100 g/4 oz caster sugar
50 g/2 oz plain flour
25 g/1 oz cocoa powder
1 tablespoon hot water
Fudge icing (see Cook's Tip)

Line and grease a 28 × 18 cm/11 × 7 inch Swiss roll tin. Whisk the eggs and sugar in a mixing bowl with an electric beater until thick enough to leave a trail. Fold in the flour, cocoa powder and water, then turn into the prepared tin. Bake in a preheated oven for 8-10 minutes until the cake springs back when lightly pressed.

Turn the sponge upside down on to sugared greaseproof paper, peel off the lining paper and trim the edges. Roll up with the sugared paper inside and allow to cool. Meanwhile make the Fudge icing. Then unroll the sponge and remove the paper, spread with some of the warm fudge icing and roll up like a Swiss roll. Leave the remaining icing to cool.

Cut a short diagonal wedge off one end of the roll and attach it to the side of the log with icing to resemble a branch. Place on a cake board. Cover the log with the cooled icing and mark lines with a fork to resemble the bark of a tree. Sprinkle with icing sugar to look like snow and add decorations.

■ COOK'S TIP

To make the Fudge icing, place 75 g/3 oz butter, 3 tablespoons milk and 2 tablespoons cocoa powder in a pan and heat gently until melted. Cool slightly, *then add 300 g/10 oz icing sugar and beat until smooth.*

134 CHAMPAGNE SORBET

Preparation time:
about 25 minutes

Cooking time:
about 5 minutes

Serves 8

Calories:
223 per portion

YOU WILL NEED:
300 g/10 oz caster sugar
250 ml/8 fl oz water
600 ml/1 pint champagne
3 tablespoons lemon juice
2 egg whites
4 tablespoons icing sugar

Dissolve the sugar in the water in a saucepan over a low heat, then bring to the boil. Boil for about 5 minutes or until the syrup is thick but not beginning to brown. Cool, then stir in 350 ml/12 fl oz of the champagne and the lemon juice. Pour into freezer trays and freeze for about 1 hour or until mushy.

Pour the mixture into a bowl and beat well for 2 minutes. Return to the freezer trays and freeze for a further 30 minutes. Beat again. Repeat the freezing and beating every 30 minutes for the next 2 hours.

Beat the egg whites until stiff. Gradually beat in the sugar. Beat the frozen mixture well to break down the ice crystals, then fold in the meringue. Return to the freezer and freeze until firm. About 30 minutes before required, transfer the sorbet to the refrigerator to soften slightly. Before serving, pour a little of the champagne over each portion.

■ COOK'S TIP

After measuring the required quantity of champagne, seal the bottle with a vacuum stopper so that the bubbles remain.

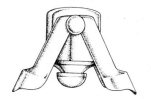

135 ICED ZABAIONE

Preparation time:
15 minutes, plus
freezing

Serves 4

Calories:
258 per portion

YOU WILL NEED:
4 egg yolks
75 g/3 oz icing sugar, sifted
4 tablespoons Marsala
6 tablespoons double cream
chopped pistachio nuts, to decorate

Place the egg yolks in a bowl with the icing sugar and whisk until thick and mousse-like. Whip the Marsala and cream together until thick, then carefully fold into the egg mixture.

Pour into 4 freezerproof ramekin dishes, cover, seal and freeze.

Sprinkle with chopped pistachio nuts to serve.

136 FRESH FRUIT WINE JELLY

Preparation time:
about 35 minutes

Serves 12

Calories:
137 per portion

YOU WILL NEED:
3 × 15 g/½ oz sachets powdered
  gelatine
300 ml/½ pint hot water
200 g/7 oz caster sugar, or to taste
juice of 2 small lemons
900 ml/1½ pints German white wine
1 kg/2¼ lb mixed fresh fruit (see
  Cook's Tip)

Dissolve the gelatine in the hot water over a pan of simmering water. Mix the dissolved gelatine with the sugar, lemon juice and wine. Cool until beginning to thicken and set.

Cut the fruit into small pieces. Put layers of fruit and jelly into a 2.25 litre/4 pint mould. The fruit will distribute itself throughout the jelly. Chill for at least 3 hours until set.

Run the tip of a knife around the edge of the mould, immerse briefly in hot water, then turn on to a flat plate. Serve with thick pouring cream and crisp dessert biscuits.

■ COOK'S TIP

If possible, use an electric mixer to whisk the egg yolks and sugar together. A rotary whisk can be used but it will take much more effort!

■ COOK'S TIP

Try to have a colourful selection of fresh fruit such as berries, oranges, grapes, bananas and cherries. Do not use either fresh pineapple or kiwi fruit because they contain an enzyme which will prevent the gelatine from setting.

137 SIMNEL CAKE

Preparation time:
about 40 minutes,
plus cooling

Cooking time:
about 2¾ hours

Oven temperature:
160 C, 325 F, gas 3
150 C, 300 F, gas 2

**Makes 1 × (18 cm/
7 inch) square cake**

Total calories: 4,914

YOU WILL NEED:
175 g/ 6 oz currants
175 g/6 oz raisins
100 g/4 oz sultanas
100 g/4 oz cut mixed peel
grated rind of 1 orange
225 g/8 oz plain flour
1 teaspoon ground cinnamon
1 teaspoon ground nutmeg
175 g/6 oz butter
175 g/6 oz soft light brown sugar
3 eggs
1 tablespoon lemon juice
500 g/18 oz marzipan
50 g/2 oz apricot jam

Combine the dried fruit, peel and rind. Sift together the flour and spices. Cream the butter and sugar until fluffy. Beat in the eggs, one at a time, alternating with a tablespoon of flour. Fold in the remaining flour and the lemon juice. Add the fruit.

Put half the mixture into a greased and lined 18 cm/7 inch square cake tin and level the top. Divide the marzipan into 3 equal portions. Roll out one piece to fit into the tin, cover with the remaining mixture and level the top. Cook in a pre-heated oven for 1 hour, then reduce the temperature and cook for a further 1¾ hours or until firm. When cold, turn out of the tin and remove the paper.

Roll out more marzipan to fit the top of the cake. Brush the top with jam, then position the marzipan. Crimp the edges. Form the remaining marzipan into 11 balls for the top. Brown lightly under a fairly low grill.

■ COOK'S TIP

To decorate this Easter-time cake, you will need about 1 metre/1 yard of yellow satin ribbon, about 3 cm/1¼ inches wide, to tie around the cake.

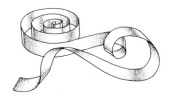

138 HOT CROSS BUNS

Preparation time:
35 minutes, plus
proving

Cooking time:
20 minutes

Oven temperature:
200 C, 400 F, gas 6

Makes 12

Calories:
215 per bun

YOU WILL NEED:
450 g/1lb plain flour
1 teaspoon salt
1 teaspoon mixed spice
2 teaspoons ground cinnamon
50 g/2 oz soft brown sugar
50 g/2 oz butter
25 g/1 oz yeast
175 ml/6 fl oz warm milk
1 large egg
75 g/3 oz currants
25 g/1 oz chopped mixed peel
FOR THE PASTE
3 tablespoons plain flour
2 tablespoons milk
1 teaspoon oil

Sift the dry ingredients into a bowl and rub in the butter. Cream the yeast with a little milk and leave until frothy. Make a well in the centre of the dry ingredients, pour in the yeast, add the egg, currants, peel and remaining milk and mix together to a smooth dough. Knead for 8 minutes. Place in a clean bowl, cover with a damp cloth and leave to rise in a warm place for 2 hours. Knead again for 2 minutes. Divide and shape into 12 buns and place on a greased baking tray. Cover and leave in a warm place for about 25 minutes.

For the paste, put the flour in a bowl and stir in the milk and oil. Spoon into a piping bag with a small nozzle and pipe a cross on the top of each bun. Bake for 20 minutes until brown. Brush with glaze (see Cook's Tip).

■ COOK'S TIP

To make the glaze, place 2 tablespoons milk and 2 tablespoons caster sugar in a small pan, bring to the boil and simmer for 2 minutes. Brush the buns *with the glaze as soon as they come out of the oven. Then transfer to a wire rack and cool slightly before serving.*

139 CHOCOLATE EASTER EGGS

Preparation time:
30-40 minutes, plus chilling

Makes 1 (15 cm/ 6 inch) egg

Total calories: 1,350

YOU WILL NEED:
225 g/8 oz plain chocolate (white or milk chocolate, optional)

Melt the chocolate in a bowl over a pan of gently simmering water and then, using a pastry brush, brush an even layer all over a mould (see Cook's Tip). Chill, then add a second layer, melting the chocolate again if necessary. Chill again and add a third coat. Chill very thoroughly, then remove the egg carefully from the mould.

If the egg is to be filled, place the chocolates inside and stick the 2 halves together with a little melted chocolate and chill once more.

If liked, pipe names and messages on these eggs using white or milk chocolate. The eggs can also be decorated with flowers made from royal icing, marzipan or fondant modelling paste.

140 EASTER TRUFFLES

Preparation time:
20 minutes, plus cooling

Makes 20

Calories:
61 per truffle

YOU WILL NEED:
175 g/6 oz plain chocolate
1 egg yolk
25 g/1 oz butter
1 teaspoon coffee-flavoured liqueur
1 tablespoon cocoa powder

Melt the chocolate in a bowl over a pan of gently simmering water. Remove from the heat and add the egg yolk, butter and liqueur. Leave in a cool place for 30-40 minutes until set.

Using your fingertips, mould into small egg shapes and roll in the cocoa powder to coat evenly.

■ COOK'S TIP

Easter egg moulds are available from specialist cake decorating and kitchen equipment shops. Plastic ones are the easiest to use as plastic separates most *readily from the chocolate egg. Plenty of time must be allowed for chilling between each application of chocolate.*

■ COOK'S TIP

Brandy, rum and other liqueurs are equally delicious flavourings. Substitute coffee essence if you prefer not to use alcohol.

141 FISH AND PRAWN TERRINE

Preparation time: 45 minutes	YOU WILL NEED: 225 g/8 oz salmon fillet
	3 tablespoons lemon juice
Cooking time: 1 hour	salt and pepper
	300 ml/½ pint water
Oven temperature: 180 C, 350 F, gas 4	1 kg/2¼ lb cod fillets, skinned
	4 egg whites
	300 ml/½ pint double cream
Serves 12	150 ml/¼ pint soured cream
Calories:	225 g/8 oz peeled cooked prawns
227 per portion	2 tablespoons chopped fresh dill

Place the salmon fillet in a small frying pan. Add 2 table-spoons of the lemon juice, salt, pepper and the water and bring to the boil. Simmer gently for 4 minutes, then remove the fish and let it cool.

Purée the cod in a food processor until smooth, then add the egg whites, double and soured creams, the remaining lemon juice and plenty of salt and pepper. Process until smooth. Spread about a quarter of the mixture evenly over the base of a lined and greased 900 g/2 lb loaf tin. Cover with 100 g/4 oz of the prawns and sprinkle over half the dill. Cover with another quarter of the cod mixture. Remove the skin from the salmon fillets and lay them on top. Cover with another quarter of the white fish mixture, top with the re-maining prawns and dill and finally spoon over the rest of the cod mixture.

Cover the terrine with a piece of greased foil and stand the tin in a roasting tin with hot water coming half-way up the sides of the tin. Cook in a preheated oven for 1 hour.

■ COOK'S TIP

To serve, carefully turn out the terrine on to a serving dish and peel off the paper. Pipe a line of thick mayonnaise down the centre, and garnish with *small spoonfuls of black lumpfish roe, whole prawns and sprigs of dill.*

142 COULIBIAC

Preparation time: about 30 minutes	YOU WILL NEED: 750 g/1½ lb salmon steaks
	50 g/2 oz butter
Cooking time: about 45 minutes	4 tablespoons dry white wine
	150 g/5 oz button mushrooms, sliced
Oven temperature: 220 C, 425 F, gas 7	1 onion, finely chopped
	450 g/1 lb frozen puff pastry, thawed
	3 hard-boiled eggs, sliced
Serves 12	100 g/4 oz brown rice, cooked
Calories:	salt and pepper
332 per portion	1 egg, lightly beaten, to glaze

Cook the salmon steaks in the butter in a large frying pan, until firm, about 5 minutes on each side. Remove from the pan and set aside. Reduce the heat, add the wine and stir in the mushrooms and onion. Cook very gently for about 5 minutes to soften. Remove from the heat. Skin and bone the fish and flake the flesh.

Roll out the pastry to a rectangle of about 38 × 30 cm/ 15 × 12 inches. Place on a baking tray. Spread layers of sal-mon, egg, rice, onion and mushroom in the centre along the length of the pastry, leaving about 4 cm/1½ inches clear at both ends. Moisten the edges of the pastry. Turn the ends in over the filling. Fold one long side over the top, then fold the second side over the first. Press along the seam. Turn the roll over so that the seam side is underneath. Glaze the pastry with the beaten egg. Pierce in a few places along the top for steam to escape. Bake in a preheated oven for 30 minutes or until well browned. Serve hot or cold.

■ COOK'S TIP

The brown rice adds a nutty texture to the filling. It absorbs more water and takes longer to cook than white rice, which can be substituted in this recipe.

143 LIME MOUSSE

Preparation time:
40 minutes, plus chilling

Cooking time:
about 15 minutes

Serves 12

Calories:
275 per portion

YOU WILL NEED:
grated rind and strained juice of 4 limes
6 eggs, separated
350 g/12 oz caster sugar
2 tablespoons water
1 teaspoon lemon juice
5 teaspoons powdered gelatine
450 ml/¾ pint whipping cream
20 frosted mint leaves (see Cook's Tip)

Place the lime rind and juice, egg yolks and sugar in a large warmed bowl. Put the bowl over a pan of gently simmering water and whisk until the mixture is thick. Place the water and lemon juice in a small basin over a pan of gently simmering water, sprinkle on the gelatine and leave until thoroughly dissolved. Allow to cool slightly, then stir evenly through the mousse mixture.

Whip 300 ml/½ pint of the cream until it is very thick but not too stiff, and fold it through the mixture. Finally whisk the egg whites until they are very stiff and dry, then fold them quickly and evenly through the mousse. Pour the mixture into a 2.25 litre/4 pint glass bowl and chill until set.

To serve, whip the remaining cream until stiff and, using a large star vegetable nozzle, pipe a row of stars around the top of the mousse. Arrange the frosted mint leaves between the stars.

144 CHAMPAGNE COCKTAILS

Preparation time:
10 minutes

Serves 12

Calories:
48 per portion

YOU WILL NEED:
12 sugar cubes
Angostura bitters
4 tablespoons lemon juice, strained
6 tablespoons brandy
2 × 70 cl bottles champagne, chilled
12 strips of lemon rind, to decorate

About 30 minutes before serving, place a sugar cube into each of 12 champagne glasses. Add a dash of bitters, 1 teaspoon lemon juice and ½ tablespoon brandy to each.

To serve, fill the glasses with champagne and decorate the edge of each glass with a small twist of lemon rind. Serve immediately.

■ COOK'S TIP

For frosted mint leaves, wash and dry the mint. Brush with lightly beaten egg white, then coat with caster sugar. Place on greaseproof paper to dry.

■ COOK'S TIP

To open a bottle of champagne, first remove the foil and wire. Grip the cork firmly in a napkin-covered hand and hold the base of the bottle equally firmly with the other hand at an angle of 45 degrees. Turn the bottle and not the cork.

145 QUAIL'S EGGS IN VERMOUTH JELLY

Preparation time:
30 minutes, plus chilling

Cooking time:
5 minutes

Serves 6

Calories:
115 per portion

YOU WILL NEED:

18 quail's eggs, boiled (see Cook's Tip)
500 ml/17 fl oz beef consommé
4 tablespoons dry vermouth
2½ teaspoons powdered gelatine
1 tablespoon chopped parsley
6 tablespoons soured cream
6 teaspoons black lumpfish roe
sprigs of parsley, to garnish

Put 3 quail's eggs into each of 6 ramekin dishes. Heat the consommé until liquid, if necessary. Put 2 tablespoons of the vermouth into a small bowl and sprinkle over the gelatine. Place the bowl over a pan of gently simmering water until the gelatine dissolves, then stir to ensure that it is thoroughly blended. Stir the gelatine mixture into the consommé with the remaining vermouth and the parsley.

Cool and then chill until the mixture begins to thicken, then pour over the eggs to fill the dishes, making sure the parsley is evenly distributed. Chill until firmly set.

To serve, put a spoonful of soured cream over each dish and spread it out a little. Top with a spoonful of lumpfish roe and a sprig of parsley. Serve with hot toast fingers or Melba toast and butter.

146 BEEF STROGANOFF

Preparation time:
15 minutes

Cooking time:
about 12 minutes

Serves 4

Calories:
366 per portion

YOU WILL NEED:

butter for frying
1 onion, finely chopped
225 g/8 oz button mushrooms, sliced
750 g/1½ lb fillet steak, cut into thin strips
salt and pepper
1 teaspoon Dijon mustard
2 tablespoons brandy
150 ml/¼ pint soured cream
chopped parsley

Melt a knob of butter in a large frying pan. Add the onion and fry for 5 minutes or until golden. Add the mushrooms and fry for a further 2 minutes.

Add the steak to the pan, season well with salt and pepper and stir in the mustard. Sauté briskly for 5 minutes or until the meat juices run pink. Stir in the brandy and soured cream and heat through gently. Adjust seasoning, transfer to a hot serving platter and sprinkle with parsley. Serve immediately.

■ COOK'S TIP

The quail's eggs can either be served soft-boiled in which case they need only 45 seconds cooking or hard-boiled when they require 4 minutes – it is simply a matter of preference. Remove from the saucepan and cool under running cold water. Remove the shells carefully.

■ COOK'S TIP

Take great care not to let the mixture boil after you add the cream or this will curdle. Buttered noodles and a green salad are suitable accompaniments.

147 ROAST PHEASANT

Preparation time: 15 minutes	**YOU WILL NEED:** 1 young pheasant, dressed and cleaned
Cooking time:	melted butter
	salt and pepper
Oven temperature: 200 C, 400 F, gas 6	4 unsmoked streaky or fat bacon rashers
Serves 4	about 600 ml/1 pint giblet stock (see recipe 130)
Calories: 537 per portion	4 rindless rashers unsmoked middle cut bacon, cut into three
	8 cocktail sausages

Wash the pheasant and dry thoroughly with absorbent kitchen paper. Brush all over with butter, then sprinkle liberally with salt and pepper. Stretch the bacon rashers with the blade of a sharp knife and use to cover the bird. Put the bird on a rack in a roasting tin and pour 450 ml/3/4 pint of the stock into the tin. Roast in a preheated oven for 40-45 minutes or until the bird is tender when pierced with a skewer, basting occasionally. Remove the bacon rashers for the last 10 minutes to brown the skin.

Twenty minutes before the end of the cooking time, roll the bacon pieces up and secure on skewers. Place on the rack around the pheasant with the sausages. When the bird is cooked, transfer to a hot serving platter. Arrange the bacon rolls around the pheasant with the sausages. Keep hot while quickly making gravy in the roasting tin (see recipe 130), adding more stock if the gravy is too thick. Serve the gravy separately in a gravy boat.

■ COOK'S TIP

Some people like to serve bread sauce with roast pheasant but crisp, butter-fried breadcrumbs are a delicious alternative, adding a contrast in texture. If you are not serving a starter, you may need 2 pheasants for 4 people.

148 CHESTNUT ROULADE

Preparation time: 25 minutes	**YOU WILL NEED:** 3 eggs, separated
	100 g/4 oz caster sugar
Cooking time: 25-30 minutes	1 × 225 g/8 oz can unsweetened chestnut purée
Oven temperature: 180 C, 350 F, gas 4	grated rind and juice of 1 orange sifted icing sugar, for sprinkling
Serves 8	300 ml/1/2 pint double cream 2 tablespoons Grand Marnier
Calories: 326 per portion	finely shredded orange rind, to decorate

Whisk the egg yolks with the sugar until thick and creamy. Put the chestnut purée in a bowl with the orange juice and beat until blended, then whisk into the egg mixture. Whisk the egg whites until fairly stiff and fold in carefully. Turn into a greased and lined 30 × 20 cm/12 × 8 inch Swiss roll tin. Bake in a preheated oven for 25-30 minutes, until firm.

Cool for 5 minutes, then cover with a damp tea-towel and leave until cold. Carefully turn the roulade on to a sheet of greaseproof paper sprinkled thickly with icing sugar. Peel off the lining paper.

Place the cream, grated orange rind and liqueur in a bowl and whip until stiff. Spread three-quarters over the roulade and roll up like a Swiss roll. Transfer to a serving dish, pipe the remaining cream along the top and decorate with shredded orange rind.

■ COOK'S TIP

Instead of using shredded orange rind to decorate the roulade, sprinkle coarsely grated plain chocolate over the top.

149 ORANGES IN CARAMEL

Preparation time:
30 minutes, plus
chilling

Cooking time:
about 10 minutes

Serves 8

Calories:
172 per portion

YOU WILL NEED:
8 juicy oranges
225 g/8 oz caster sugar
300 ml/½ pint water

Remove the outer rind from 2 of the oranges with a sharp knife and cut into thin matchstick strips. Put in a small pan of water, bring to the boil and simmer for 5 minutes. Drain and refresh under cold running water. Set aside. Remove the peel and pith from all the oranges. Put in a large glass serving bowl and set aside.

Put the sugar and half the water in a saucepan over a gentle heat. When the sugar has dissolved, increase the heat and boil until the syrup turns a rich brown, caramel colour. Remove the pan from the heat and immediately pour in the remaining water, being careful to avoid any splashing. Return the pan to the heat and dissolve the caramel over a very gentle heat. Remove from the heat and leave to cool before pouring over the oranges. Sprinkle with the orange rind and chill before serving.

150 PUMPKIN PIE

Preparation time:
20 minutes, plus
chilling

Cooking time:
45 minutes, plus
resting

Oven temperature:
200 C, 400 F, gas 6

Serves 8

Calories:
449 per portion

YOU WILL NEED:
225 g/8 oz plain flour
pinch of salt
50 g/2 oz lard
50 g/2 oz butter, diced
2 tablespoons cold water
whipped cream, to serve
FOR THE FILLING
1 × 400 g/14 oz can pumpkin purée
175 g/6 oz caster sugar
1 tablespoon cornflour
1 tablespoon black treacle
2 teaspoons mixed spice
150 ml/¼ pint single cream
3 eggs, well beaten

Place the flour and salt in a bowl. Rub in the fat until the mixture resembles fine breadcrumbs. Add the water and mix to form a fairly firm dough. Knead lightly. Wrap in cling film and chill for at least 15 minutes.

Roll out the pastry fairly thinly on a floured board and use to line the base and sides of a 23 cm/9 inch, lightly greased, fluted flan dish. To make the filling, put all the ingredients into a mixing bowl and beat with a wooden spoon until thoroughly combined. Pour the mixture into the pastry case.

Bake in a preheated oven for 45 minutes, then open the oven door, turn off the heat and leave the pie in the oven for a further 15 minutes.

■ COOK'S TIP

Cutting the peeled oranges into slices will help this recipe go further. Remove any pips from the slices.

■ COOK'S TIP

This pie is traditionally quite sweet, so serve it in small portions, still warm from the oven. Top each portion with a spoonful of whipped cream. Replace the *mixed spice in the pie filling with cinnamon, if preferred.*

151 WEST COUNTRY FONDUE

Preparation time:
15 minutes

Cooking time:
about 8 minutes

Serves 6

Calories:
334 per portion

YOU WILL NEED:
½ small onion, cut
300 ml/½ pint dry cider
1 teaspoon lemon juice
450 g/1 lb Farmhouse Cheddar cheese,
     grated
1 tablespoon cornflour
2 tablespoons sherry
pinch of mustard powder
1 teaspoon Worcestershire sauce
pepper

Rub the inside of a flameproof dish with the cut side of the onion. Add the cider and lemon juice and heat until bubbling. Gradually stir in the cheese and heat gently, stirring continuously, until it melts and begins to cook.

Blend in the cornflour with the sherry and add the mustard, Worcestershire sauce and pepper to taste. Add to the cheese and continue to heat, stirring, for 2-3 minutes until the mixture is thick and creamy. Serve immediately, with French bread.

152 MULLED RED WINE

Preparation time:
10-15 minutes

Cooking time:
about 30 minutes

Makes about 60 glasses

Calories:
104 per glass

YOU WILL NEED:
8-9 bottles red wine
350 g/12 oz raisins
450 g/1 lb caster sugar
4 cinnamon sticks
thinly pared rind of 1 lemon
thinly pared rind of 1 orange
20 whole cloves
2.25 litres/4 pints boiling water
450 ml/¾ pint brandy
2 lemons, thinly sliced
2 oranges, thinly sliced

Put the wine into a large saucepan or preserving pan. Add the raisins, sugar, cinnamon sticks, lemon and orange rinds and cloves. Bring to the boil slowly, stirring continuously until all the sugar has dissolved. Simmer very gently for 20-25 minutes, stirring occasionally. Add the water and brandy and bring just back to the boil. Add the slices of lemon and orange. At this stage the mixture may be cooled and reheated when you are ready to serve.

Ladle into glasses, putting a silver spoon into each one before you pour the wine. (Pouring the hot liquid over silver prevents glasses from cracking or breaking.)

▮ COOK'S TIP

Always heat the cider before adding the cheese. Stir the fondue in a figure of eight motion – this helps to blend the cheese into the cider. Keep the heat low. If the fondue curdles, add a few drops of lemon juice, heat and stir vigorously.

▮ COOK'S TIP

The boxes of wine available from most supermarkets and off-licences are suitable for mulling. Use the least expensive brandy you can find.

153 ARTICHAUTS AVEC MOUSSELINE DE CAVIARE

Preparation time:
30 minutes, plus chilling

Cooking time:
30 minutes

Serves 4

Calories:
345 per portion

YOU WILL NEED:
4 globe artichokes (see Cook's Tip)
salt and pepper
2 tablespoons white wine vinegar
150 ml/1/4 pint olive oil
2 tablespoons lemon juice
1 garlic clove, crushed
FOR THE MOUSSELINE
150 ml/1/4 pint soured cream
1 teaspoon grated lemon rind
1 tablespoon finely chopped parsley
75 g/3 oz red lumpfish roe, plus extra
to garnish

Bring a large pan of water to the boil and add a teaspoon of salt and the wine vinegar. Add the prepared artichokes, right way up, and cook steadily for about 30 minutes. Meanwhile, combine the oil, lemon juice and garlic for the dressing, adding salt and pepper to taste.

Drain the cooked artichokes thoroughly. Turn the artichokes the right way up. Twist and pull out the central cone of leaves in each one and reserve, exposing the hairy choke. Scrape out the choke with a small spoon. Stand the artichokes upright on a dish and spoon the dressing over the artichokes and reserved leaves. Tip the artichokes so that any excess dressing drips off. Stand the artichokes upright on 4 serving dishes, surrounded by the reserved leaves.

Mix together the mousseline ingredients; spoon into the centres of the artichokes. Garnish with extra roe.

■ COOK'S TIP

Cut off the top quarter of each artichoke. Snap off the stalks and trim the ends so that the artichokes will sit level. Rub the cut surfaces with a lemon half to prevent discoloration. Check if the artichokes are cooked by removing an outside lower leaf; if the fleshy base is tender, then the artichoke is cooked.

154 ZARZUELA

Preparation time:
about 35 minutes

Cooking time:
about 30 minutes

Serves 6

Calories:
319 per portion

YOU WILL NEED:
300 ml/1/2 pint dry white wine
2 garlic cloves, finely chopped
3 tablespoons chopped parsley
1 litre/ 1³/4 pints mussels, cleaned
6 large Mediterranean prawns
1 onion, finely chopped
3 tablespoons olive oil
750 g/1¹/2 lb tomatoes, skinned, seeded
    and chopped
1 teaspoon powdered saffron
50 g/2 oz blanched almonds, chopped
salt and pepper
1 medium lobster, cooked and halved
450 g/1 lb sole fillets, cut into strips
175 g/6 oz peeled cooked prawns
3 tablespoons brandy

Put the wine, garlic and parsley into a large pan and bring to the boil. Add the mussels and large prawns; cover the pan and simmer for 5 minutes. Remove the shellfish, reserving their cooking liquid. Discard any unopened mussels. Gently fry the chopped onion in the olive oil in a large shallow pan for 3-4 minutes. Add the tomatoes and cook until soft and pulpy. Add the saffron, almonds, salt and pepper, and the shellfish cooking liquid. Simmer gently for 10 minutes.

Add the prepared lobster (see Cook's Tip) and the sole to the sauce and simmer 3 minutes. Add the mussels in their shells, the large prawns, peeled prawns and lobster meat. Simmer 3-4 minutes. Stir in the brandy and serve.

■ COOK'S TIP

To prepare the lobster, discard the stomach sac, grey spongy gills and intestinal vein. Cut the meat into bite-sized pieces.

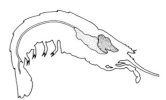

155 ARROZ A LA MARINIERA

Preparation time:
about 40 minutes

Cooking time:
about 30 minutes

Serves 6

Calories:
452 per portion

YOU WILL NEED:
6 tablespoons olive oil
175 g/6 oz monkfish, cut into chunks
175 g/6 oz prepared squid (see Cook's Tip)
1 large onion, finely chopped
6 tomatoes, skinned, seeded and chopped
2 teaspoons paprika pepper
1 large garlic clove, crushed
salt
350 g/12 oz Valencia rice (or small round-grain rice)
900 ml/1½ pints fish or chicken stock
450 ml/¾ pint mussels, scrubbed and bearded
175 g/6 oz peeled cooked prawns, cleaned but left whole
100 g/4 oz lobster, in large flakes

Heat the oil in a deep frying pan. Add the monkfish and squid and fry until golden. Add the onion, tomatoes, paprika, garlic and salt to taste. Cook, stirring, for 1-2 minutes. Add the rice and the stock. Simmer gently for 5 minutes without stirring.

Lay the mussels and prawns on top of the rice and continue cooking for a further 15 minutes. Remove and discard any mussels that have not opened. Lay the lobster on top of the other ingredients and cook for a further 5 minutes. By this time the rice should be tender and the liquid absorbed. Stir the seafood into the rice.

▮ COOK'S TIP

To prepare squid, cut off the head with the tentacles attached, just above the eyes, and reserve; pull what is left of the head out of the body, along with the transparent backbone. Rinse the body and slide off the outer skin and fins. Use the fins and tentacles as they are, cut the body into rings.

156 HALVA

Preparation time:
5 minutes, plus chilling

Cooking time:
20-25 minutes

Makes about 36 pieces

Calories:
166 per piece

YOU WILL NEED:
250 ml/8 fl oz olive oil
500 g/18 oz fine semolina
450 g/1 lb sugar
750 ml/1¼ pints milk
250 ml/8 fl oz dry Greek white wine
ground cinnamon, for dusting

Heat the oil in a large shallow frying pan over a gentle heat. Pour in the semolina in a fine, steady stream, stirring continuously. Cook gently, stirring occasionally, until all the oil has been absorbed and the semolina is pale golden. Stir in the sugar, milk and white wine. Cook for 10 minutes, stirring continuously, until the mixture is thick and will hold its shape on a wooden spoon (take care that it does not burn).

Pour into a lightly greased shallow rectangular dish or tin 30 × 20 cm/12 × 8 inches (or use 2 smaller tins if preferred) and level off the surface. Chill for about 4 hours until firm. Dust lightly with cinnamon and cut into squares.

▮ COOK'S TIP

Homemade halva can be stored in the refrigerator for up to 3 days. Serve it with strong black coffee after a Mediterranean-style dinner.

157 FISH MOLEE

Preparation time:
25 minutes

Cooking time:
15-20 minutes

Serves 4

Calories:
317 per portion

YOU WILL NEED:
750 g/1½ lb cod fillet, skinned and cut
  into 4 pieces
2 tablespoons plain flour
4 tablespoons oil
2 onions, sliced
2 garlic cloves, crushed
1 teaspoon turmeric
4 green chillies, finely chopped
2 tablespoons lemon juice
175 ml/6 fl oz thick coconut milk (see
  Cook's Tip)
salt

Coat the fish with the flour. Heat the oil in a frying pan, add
the fish and fry quickly on both sides. Remove with a slotted
spoon and set aside.

Add the onion and garlic to the pan and fry until soft and
golden. Add the turmeric, chillies, lemon juice, coconut milk,
and salt to taste and simmer, uncovered, for 10 minutes or
until thickened.

Add the fish and any juices, spoon over the sauce and
cook gently for 2-3 minutes, until tender.

158 DHAI BHINDI

Preparation time:
15 minutes

Cooking time:
15 minutes

Serves 4

Calories:
99 per portion

YOU WILL NEED:
225 g/8 oz okra
2 tablespoons oil
2.5 cm/1 inch piece root ginger,
  chopped
1 teaspoon turmeric (see Cook's Tip)
salt
2-3 tablespoons water
300 ml/½ pint natural yogurt
½ teaspoon chilli powder
2 tablespoons grated coconut
1 tablespoon finely chopped coriander
  leaves

Cut the tops off the okra and halve them lengthways. Heat the
oil in a pan, add the okra and fry for 5 minutes. Add the ginger, turmeric, and salt to taste, stir well, add the water, cover
and cook for 10 minutes, until the okra is tender.

Mix the remaining ingredients together; add to the pan,
stir well and serve.

■ COOK'S TIP

*To make coconut milk,
place 225 g/8 oz grated
coconut in a bowl, pour
over about 600 ml/1 pint
boiling water, just to cover
and leave for 1 hour. Strain
through muslin, squeezing
hard to extract as much
'thick' milk as possible.
Creamed coconut is a useful
substitute.*

■ COOK'S TIP

*Turmeric is a rhizome
commonly used in its
powdered form for its
earthy taste and yellow
colour. It stains clothing
and work surfaces.*

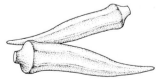

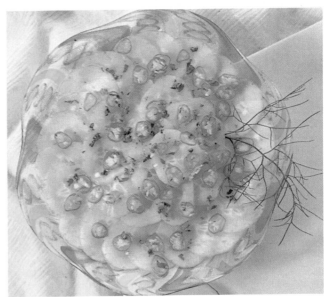

159 KASHMIRI CHICKEN

Preparation time:
20 minutes

Cooking time:
35-40 minutes

Serves 4

Calories:
525 per portion

YOU WILL NEED:
100 g/4 oz butter
3 large onions, finely sliced
10 peppercorns
10 cardamom (see Cook's Tip)
5 cm/2 inch piece cinnamon stick
5 cm/2 inch piece root ginger chopped
1-2 garlic cloves, finely chopped
1 teaspoon chilli powder
2 teaspoons paprika
salt
1 kg/2¼ lb chicken pieces, skinned
175 ml/6 fl oz natural yogurt

Melt the butter in a deep, lidded frying pan. Add the onions, peppercorns, cardamom and cinnamon and fry until the onions are golden. Add the ginger, garlic, chilli powder, paprika and salt to taste and fry for 2 minutes, stirring occasionally. Add the chicken pieces and fry until browned. Gradually add the yogurt, stirring constantly. Cover and cook gently for about 30 minutes. Remove and discard the cinnamon stick and cardamom pods before serving.

160 ZALATA

Preparation time:
15 minutes, plus
draining and
chilling

Serves 4

Calories:
10 per portion

YOU WILL NEED:
225 g/8 oz ridge cucumbers, peeled
and sliced
salt
1 green chilli, sliced
1 tablespoon finely chopped coriander
leaves
2 tablespoons vinegar
½ teaspoon caster sugar

Put the cucumber into a colander, sprinkle with salt and leave to drain for 30 minutes. Dry thoroughly with absorbent kitchen paper. Place in a serving dish and add the remaining ingredients and 1 teaspoon salt. Mix well and chill thoroughly before serving.

Alternatively, put the drained cucumber into a blender or food processor with the whole chilli, coriander leaves, sugar and salt. Add 1 garlic clove and just 1½ teaspoons vinegar and work to a smooth paste. Chill thoroughly before serving.

■ COOK'S TIP

Cardamom (elaichi) is an aromatic seed pod which comes in three varieties: white, green (more perfumed that the white) and large black (not always available). The whole pod is used to flavour rice and meat dishes and then discarded, or the pod is opened and the seeds removed and crushed.

■ COOK'S TIP

Use hot green chillies with care. For a less pungent flavour discard the seeds. Do not touch your face or rub your eyes while handling chillies.

Buffet Parties

Visual impact is important at buffet parties: choose recipes which will offer a variety of textures and shapes. Have two or three main dishes, including a non-meat one, so that each dish does not have to contain enough servings to cater for all the guests at the party.

161 Open Sandwiches

Preparation time:
allow 30 minutes

Serves:
allow 1 per person

YOU WILL NEED:
white bread
brown bread
French bread
rye bread
crispbreads
butter
toppings (see method)
cheeses (see method)
garnishes (see method)

These are ideal for small buffet parties. Use any of the bread bases listed above, spread with butter. Place a slice of one of the cheeses listed below on top. Select a topping and one or more of the suggested garnishes to complement the cheese in flavour, but provide contrast in colour.

Toppings: sliced cold meats, salami, pâté, chicken, sardines, prawns.

Cheeses: Cheddar, Leicester, Double Gloucester, Edam, Gouda, Emmental, Gruyère, Jarlsberg, Danish blue vein, Blue Stilton, cottage cheese, cream cheese.

Garnishes: onion rings, parsley, cucumber twists, watercress, tomatoes, gherkin fans, olives, sliced hard-boiled eggs, red pepper slices, shredded lettuce, caviar or lumpfish roe, pineapple, orange slices, fresh herbs.

162 Vol-au-vents

Preparation time:
25 minutes

Cooking time:
(see method)

Oven temperature:
(see method)

Makes 36 cases

Calories:
117 per portion

YOU WILL NEED:
36 medium frozen vol-au-vent cases
FOR THE 3 FILLINGS
225 g/8 oz full fat soft cheese
1 teaspoon tomato purée
1 large ripe avocado
2-3 teaspoons lemon juice
salt and pepper
3 eggs, hard-boiled
2-3 tablespoons mayonnaise
FOR THE GARNISH
2 slices smoked salmon
1 canned red pimento
few bottled or canned button
  mushrooms

Bake the vol-au-vent cases according to the manufacturer's instructions.

Make the fillings. Beat together the cheese and the tomato purée. Peel the avocado and mash with a fork. Beat in lemon juice to taste and season well. Mash the eggs finely and mix to a smooth cream with mayonnaise. Season.

Prepare the garnishes. Cut the smoked salmon into narrow strips and curl into coils. Cut the pimento into tiny shapes with aspic cutters or a sharp knife.

To assemble the vol-au-vents, divide the prepared fillings between the baked pastry cases. Top the cheese filling with smoked salmon coils, the egg filling with button mushrooms and the avocado filling with pimento pieces. Alternatively, lumpfish roe may be used to garnish the egg vol-au-vents.

■ COOK'S TIP

Open sandwiches look impressive arranged on a tray. Provide a cake slice to enable guests to lift the sandwiches off the tray and on to individual plates.

■ COOK'S TIP

These fillings and garnishes would also work very well with small shortcrust pastry tart cases. Fill the pastry tarts just before serving.

163 CRISPY CHEESE FRIES

Preparation time:
10 minutes, plus
chilling

Cooking time:
15-20 minutes

Serves 12

Calories:
339 per portion

YOU WILL NEED:
100 g/4 oz butter
100 g/4 oz plain flour
900 ml/1½ pints milk
salt and pepper
freshly grated nutmeg
350 g/12 oz Gruyère cheese, grated
4 tablespoons grated Parmesan cheese
2 × 175 g/6 oz cans crabmeat, drained
    and flaked
4 egg yolks, beaten
2 eggs
4 tablespoons milk
fresh breadcrumbs for coating
oil for deep-frying
fried parsley sprigs, to garnish

Melt the butter in a pan, stir in the flour and cook for 2
minutes. Gradually add the milk, stirring constantly. Bring to
the boil, and add salt, pepper and nutmeg to taste.Add the
cheeses and stir until melted.

Remove from the heat and mix in the crabmeat and egg
yolks. Spread the mixture in a shallow baking tin to a 1 cm/½
inch thickness. Cover with foil and chill for 3-4 hours.

Cut the paste into rectangles, about 4 cm/1½ inches long.
Beat the eggs with the milk. Dip the cheese cubes into the egg
mixture, then into the breadcrumbs to coat evenly. Heat the
oil in a deep-fryer to 190 C/375 F and fry the cheese cubes in
batches until crisp, and golden. Garnish with the parsley
before serving.

■ COOK'S TIP

*These cheese fries will keep
happily in a moderate oven
for 30 minutes or so before
serving. Keep them in the
centre of the oven rather
than near the top.*

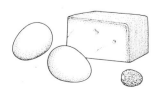

164 KRISPROLLS WITH SALAMI CONES

Preparation time:
20 minutes

Makes 10

Calories:
70 per portion

YOU WILL NEED:
10 krisprolls
butter, for spreading
10 slices salami
175 g/6 oz full fat cream cheese
1 tablespoon thick mayonnaise
1 teaspoon lemon juice
good pinch of celery salt
freshly ground black pepper
10 small leafy celery sticks

Spread each krisproll with butter and stand it on a platter.
Roll each slice of salami into a cone.

Cream the cheese with the mayonnaise, lemon juice, celery salt and add pepper to taste. Put the mixture into a piping
bag fitted with a large star nozzle and pipe a large whirl into
each salami cone.

Push a small leafy stick of celery into each salami cone
and lay one on each krisproll, attaching it to the butter.

■ COOK'S TIP

*Make the salami cones in
advance and keep them in
the refrigerator, covered
with cling film, until
required. The cones may be
put on the krisprolls 30* *minutes or so before
serving.*

165 ARDENNES PATE

Preparation time:
25 minutes, plus
chilling

Cooking time:
1½ hours

Oven temperature:
180 C, 350 F, gas 4

Serves 16

Calories:
231 per portion

YOU WILL NEED:
450 g/1 lb pork fillet, diced
450 g/1 lb belly pork, diced
450 g/1 lb minced veal
750 g/1½ lb chicken livers, chopped
(see Cook's Tip)
8 tablespoons brandy
4 teaspoons chopped thyme
2 tablespoons green peppercorns
salt and pepper
8-12 rashers rindless streaky bacon
FOR THE GARNISH
thyme sprigs
lemon slices

Combine the pork, veal and chicken livers in a large bowl. Stir in the brandy, thyme, peppercorns, and salt and pepper to taste. Cover and chill for 2 hours.

Spoon the mixture into a lightly greased 1 kg/2 lb loaf tin. Stretch the bacon and use to cover the pâté. Cover with foil and place in a roasting pan. Pour in enough boiling water to come halfway up the sides of the pan. Cook in a preheated oven for 1½ hours.

Leave the pâté to cool in the tin; turn out when cold. Garnish with thyme and lemon slices, and serve with toast, crispbread or crackers.

166 CHICKEN LIVER PATE

Preparation time:
20 minutes

Cooking time:
2¼-2¾ hours

Oven temperature:
150 C, 300 F, gas 2

Serves 12

Calories:
273 per portion

YOU WILL NEED:
100 g/4 oz butter
225 g/8 oz rindless back bacon,
chopped
4 garlic cloves, crushed
2 small onions, chopped
1 kg/2 lb chicken livers, chopped
salt and pepper
4 thyme sprigs
4 parsley sprigs
225 g/8 oz button mushrooms,
chopped
120 ml/4 fl oz dry sherry
120 ml/4 fl oz double cream
2 teaspoons lemon juice
watercress sprigs

Melt the butter in a large pan, add the bacon, garlic and onion and cook gently for 3 minutes. Stir in the chicken livers and cook for 5 minutes. Season liberally with salt and pepper. Stir in the herbs and mushrooms. Add the sherry and cook until the liquid has evaporated. Cool, then work in an electric blender until smooth. Stir in the cream and lemon juice.

Spoon into a greased ovenproof dish. Cover with a lid and stand in a roasting pan, containing water to a depth of 2.5 cm/1 inch. Bake in a preheated oven for 2-2½ hours, until cooked through. Allow to cool. Cover and chill until required.

Garnish with watercress, and serve with hot toast, French bread or crispbread.

■ COOK'S TIP

If frozen chicken livers are used for this recipe, they will chop more easily and neatly if the chopping is done while they are still a little frozen. Thaw the

chopped livers completely before adding them to the rest of the ingredients.

■ COOK'S TIP

This pâté will keep well in the refrigerator for at least a week – and for several weeks if it is completely sealed with a layer of lard or clarified butter on top.

167 MUSHROOMS ITALIENNE

Preparation time:
15 minutes, plus
marinating

Cooking time:
2-3 minutes

Serves 10

Calories:
194 per portion

YOU WILL NEED:
8 shelled scallops
8 tablespoons dry white wine
2 parsley sprigs
½ small onion
strip of lemon rind
225 g/8 oz peeled prawns
450 g/1 lb button mushrooms, thinly
   sliced
175 ml/6 fl oz olive oil
4 tablespoons lemon or lime juice
1 garlic clove, crushed
2 teaspoons chopped parsley
salt and pepper
few lettuce leaves

Separate the coral from the white scallop meat then slice the scallops.

Put the wine, parsley sprigs, onion and lemon rind into a pan, add the scallops (including the coral) and cook for 2 minutes.

Using a slotted spoon, lift out the fish and put into a bowl. Leave to cool, then stir in the prawns.

Put the mushrooms into another bowl and pour over the oil and lemon or lime juice. Sprinkle with the garlic, parsley and plenty of pepper. Toss well and leave to stand for 30 minutes. Stir in a little salt, add to the fish and stir well.

Arrange the lettuce leaves on individual serving dishes and pile the mushroom mixture on top. Cover and chill until required.

■ COOK'S TIP

Alert guests to the fact that this mushroom salad contains scallops by serving it on scallop shells rather than in individual dishes.

168 MARINATED STUFFED MUSHROOMS

Preparation time:
30 minutes, plus
marinating

Serves 10

Calories:
196 per portion

YOU WILL NEED:
40 button mushrooms, total weight
   about 450 g/1 lb
5 tablespoons safflower or sunflower
   oil
4 tablespoons dry white wine
salt and pepper
1 garlic clove, crushed
FOR THE FILLING
175 g/6 oz chicken liver pâté
75 g/3 oz butter, softened
75 g/3 oz full fat soft cream cheese
3 tablespoons chopped fresh parsley
sliced stuffed olives or small pieces of
   pickled walnut, to garnish

Remove the stems from the mushrooms and wipe them.

Whisk the oil, wine, salt, pepper and garlic together in a bowl. Add the mushrooms and mix to coat them evenly with the dressing. Cover and leave to marinate for 1-2 hours, stirring occasionally.

To make the filling, cream together the pâté, butter and cream cheese until evenly blended, then beat in the parsley and add salt and pepper. Put the filling into a piping bag fitted with a large star vegetable nozzle.

Drain the mushrooms, turning them upside-down on absorbent kitchen paper, then pipe a whirl of the pâté and cheese mixture into each cup. Top each mushroom with a slice of stuffed olive or a piece of pickled walnut.

■ COOK'S TIP

To turn this recipe into a first course for a more formal meal, choose large, flat cap mushrooms and allow 1 per person. The amount of marinade here should be sufficient for 6 large mushrooms and the mushrooms would need the full 2 hours' marinating time.

169 MEXICAN DIP WITH CRUDITES

Preparation time:
15 minutes

Serves 10

Calories:
228 per portion

YOU WILL NEED:
4 ripe avocado pears
juice of 1 lemon
4 tomatoes
1 small onion, grated
1 garlic clove, crushed
1 teaspoon Worcestershire sauce
120 ml/4 fl oz natural yogurt
salt and pepper
1 small cauliflower
8 carrots
8 celery sticks
1 cucumber
4 green or red peppers

Halve the avocados and remove the stones. Scoop the flesh into a bowl and mash with the lemon juice. Skin, seed and chop the tomatoes and add to the bowl with the onion, garlic, Worcestershire sauce, yogurt and salt and pepper to taste. Beat thoroughly until smooth and divide between 2 serving dishes.

Break the cauliflower into florets and cut the remaining vegetables into matchstick pieces, discarding the core and seeds from the peppers.

Place each dish on a large plate and surround with the vegetables.

170 PORKY MEATBALLS WITH MANGO DIP

Preparation time:
about 30 minutes

Cooking time:
about 25 minutes

Makes 40

Calories:
59 per portion

YOU WILL NEED:
1 kg/2 lb finely minced pork
2 onions, minced
½ teaspoon dried marjoram
½ teaspoon ground coriander
3 tablespoons plain flour
2 eggs, beaten
salt and pepper
oil or fat for deep frying
FOR THE MANGO DIP
6 tablespoons French dressing
8 tablespoons mango chutney
2 teaspoons lemon juice
2 tablespoons soured cream

Combine the pork, onions, herbs, coriander, flour and eggs, season with salt and pepper, and beat until smooth. Form into 40 balls about the size of a small walnut (see Cook's Tip).

Heat the oil to 180 C/350 F or until a cube of bread will brown in about 30 seconds. Fry the meatballs, a few at a time, for about 4 minutes until golden brown. Drain on absorbent kitchen paper and keep warm.

To make the mango dip, put all the ingredients into a food processor or mixer and blend until thoroughly emulsified and almost smooth. Turn the dip into a bowl and stand the bowl on a large plate.

When you are ready to serve, arrange the meatballs around the bowl of mango dip, spearing each one with a cocktail stick ready for guests to help themselves.

■ COOK'S TIP

This tangy version of Guacamole can also be used as a filling for celery sticks, pastry cases, or small cases made from rounds of oiled bread baked in the oven.

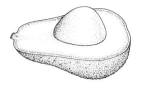

■ COOK'S TIP

Keep a bowl of plain flour by the meatball mixture and use it to keep the fingers lightly dusted while making the meatballs. This prevents the mixture sticking.

171 MONKFISH BITES WITH MINT DIP

Preparation time:
25 minutes, plus
marinating

Cooking time:
about 10 minutes

Serves 20

Calories:
109 per portion

YOU WILL NEED:
4 tablespoons lemon juice
4 tablespoons oil
2 teaspoons white wine vinegar
salt and pepper
1 onion, very finely chopped
1 tablespoon chopped fresh mint
1 kg/2 lb monkfish
FOR THE MINT DIP
3 tablespoons thick mayonnaise
3 tablespoons thick set natural yogurt
1 teaspoon lemon juice
2 tablespoons chopped fresh mint
½ teaspoon caster sugar
sprig of mint, to garnish

In a bowl combine the lemon juice, oil, vinegar, salt, pepper, onion and mint.

Cut the monkfish into 2.5 cm/1 inch cubes, making sure all the skin and bone is removed. Add the fish to the marinade, cover, and leave to stand in a cool place for 2 hours.

To make the dip, mix together all the ingredients and season to taste with salt and pepper. Spoon the dip into a small bowl, cover with cling film and chill.

To serve, drain the pieces of fish and thread them on to long skewers. Cook under a preheated moderate grill for about 5 minutes on each side until they are cooked through. Stand the dip in the centre of a plate, garnish with a sprig of mint, and arrange the pieces of monkfish around it.

 COOK'S TIP

Try to serve the monkfish bites as freshly cooked as possible. Ideally they should be grilled about 30 minutes before the party is due to start.

172 PILAFF

Preparation time:
10 minutes

Cooking time:
about 20 minutes

Serves 30

Calories:
191 per portion

YOU WILL NEED:
150 ml/¼ pint sunflower oil
1 kg/2 lb long-grain rice
1 litre/1¾ pints water
4 teaspoons salt
450 g/1 lb onions, chopped
6 fat garlic cloves, sliced
100 g/4 oz blanched whole almonds
100 g/4 oz raisins
450 g/1 lb tomatoes, skinned, seeded and chopped

Heat 5 tablespoons of the oil in a large pan and add the rice, water and salt. Bring to the boil, cover tightly and simmer for about 15 minutes, until the liquid is absorbed and the rice is tender.

Meanwhile, heat the remaining oil in another pan, add the onions, garlic and almonds and fry until golden. Add the raisins and tomatoes and cook for 5 minutes.

Transfer the rice to a large warmed serving dish, flaking with a fork to separate the grains. Pour the onion and tomato mixture from the pan over the rice and mix in with a fork until well blended. Serve hot.

COOK'S TIP

If this Pilaff is cooked in advance of the meal, keep it hot, tightly covered with foil, in a moderate oven.

173 BAKED FISH

Preparation time:
20 minutes

Cooking time:
about 45 minutes

Oven temperature:
180 C, 350 F, gas 4

Serves 8

Calories:
313 per portion

YOU WILL NEED:
*1 × 1.5 kg/3 lb fish (grey mullet,
   salmon, salmon trout), cleaned*
1 small onion, finely chopped
325 ml/11 fl oz white wine
50 g/2 oz butter, melted
FOR THE GARNISH
1-2 canned pimentos
*strips of thinly pared lemon rind, lime
   rind and cucumber peel*
*sprigs fresh herbs (tarragon, chives,
   chervil)*

Rinse out the fish thoroughly with cold water. Line a roasting tin with foil and make 2-3 diagonal slashes across the thickest part of the fish flesh on both sides. Arrange the fish in the tin.

Spoon the onion and 4 tablespoons of wine over the fish, then spoon the butter over. Wrap the head and tail of the fish with foil to prevent them drying.

Bake for about 45 minutes, basting once or twice, until the flesh is opaque (test by inserting a knife into the thickest part, near the bone), and the skin rubs off easily.

Transfer the fish to a serving platter and allow to cool.

When completely cold, decorate the fish. Cut the pimentos, lemon and lime rind and cucumber peel into shapes and strips using a sharp knife. Arrange around or on the fish with the herbs.

174 CHILLI CHICKEN DRUMSTICKS

Preparation time:
20 minutes, plus
marinating

Cooking time:
about 20 minutes

Serves 10

Calories:
234 per portion

YOU WILL NEED:
2 tablespoons oil
1 onion, finely chopped
1 garlic clove, crushed
150 ml/¼ pint tomato ketchup
3 tablespoons Worcestershire sauce
2-3 teaspoons chilli seasoning
150 ml/¼ pint red wine vinegar
2 tablespoons apricot jam
1 teaspoon dry mustard
20 chicken drumsticks
sprigs of parsley, to garnish

Heat the oil in a pan and fry the onion and garlic until soft, then continue frying until lightly coloured.

Add the ketchup, Worcestershire sauce, chilli seasoning, vinegar, jam and mustard and bring slowly to the boil. Simmer gently for 2 minutes, remove from the heat and let cool.

Arrange the drumsticks in a roasting tin or on a large platter in a single layer and pour the sauce over them. Leave to marinate in a cool place for at least 3 hours, turning the chicken occasionally.

When you are ready to cook, drain the marinade from the drumsticks and reserve, and put the drumsticks under a preheated moderately hot grill. Cook for 8 minutes on each side until they are cooked right through and well browned. Put on to a platter, garnish and keep warm.

Heat the reserved marinade in a saucepan and serve with the drumsticks.

■ COOK'S TIP

Ideally, this fish should be served as soon as possible after decorating. Putting it on the buffet table ready cut through into steaks or slices will help portion control.

■ COOK'S TIP

These drumsticks may also be cooked in a preheated hot oven (220 C, 425 F, gas 7) for about 40 minutes, turning once. They are also a good barbecue dish, *needing about 8 minutes each side on a moderately hot barbecue.*

175 PORK AND VEAL GALANTINE

Preparation time:
25 minutes

Cooking time:
1¾ hours

Oven temperature:
180 C, 350 F, gas 4

Serves 12

Calories:
196 per portion

YOU WILL NEED:
vegetable oil for brushing
750 g/1½ lb minced veal
750 g/1½ lb minced pork
1 large onion, grated
3 large garlic cloves, crushed
3 tablespoons chopped fresh parsley
2 teaspoons crushed dried rosemary
salt and pepper
2 eggs, beaten
about 175 g/6 oz rindless streaky
   bacon rashers
100 g/4 oz button mushrooms, sliced

Cut out a sheet of foil approximately 46 cm/18 inches square and brush with oil, leaving a 5cm/2 inch border all round.

Combine the meats, onion, garlic and herbs. Season well. Mix in the eggs then spread over the oiled part of the foil.

Stretch the bacon rashers with the back of a knife. Press the mushrooms on to the surface of the meat. Roll the meat up like a Swiss roll with the mushrooms inside, using the foil to support the mixture. Wrap the bacon rashers around the roll, tucking the ends firmly underneath. Gently roll again until evenly shaped. Wrap the roll tightly in the foil then place on a baking tray, diagonally, if necessary.

Bake for 1½ hours, then open the foil and cook for a further 15 minutes. Pour off any meat juices and allow to cool. Re-wrap the galantine and chill in the refrigerator for up to 24 hours.

◼ COOK'S TIP

This galantine may be served either hot or cold. If it is to be served cold, slice it thinly and serve with assorted salads. Serve it hot with vegetables and a tomato sauce. The cooked and cooled galantine may also be frozen for one month (thaw in its wrapping at room temperature for 4 hours).

176 SAVOURY ROULADE

Preparation time:
25 minutes

Cooking time:
50-55 minutes

Oven temperature:
160 C, 325 F, gas 3

Serves 8

Calories:
308 per portion

YOU WILL NEED:
450 g/1 lb parsnips or celeriac
salt and pepper
50 g/2 oz butter
3 tablespoons plain flour
large pinch of ground mace
3 eggs, separated
1 medium onion, finely chopped
1 tablespoon lemon juice
2 ripe avocados, peeled and mashed
150 g/5 oz full fat soft cheese

Grease and line a 28 × 20 cm/11 × 8 inch Swiss roll tin.

Cook the parsnips in boiling salted water until tender. Drain, reserving the cooking liquid. Mash the parsnips, purée, then sieve. Make up to 450 ml/¾ pint with the liquid.

Melt the butter in a saucepan over a low heat. Stir in the flour and cook for 1-2 minutes. Gradually stir in the vegetable purée and cook, stirring continuously, for about 3 minutes until thickened. Remove from the heat and add salt, pepper and mace. Beat in the egg yolks. Whisk the egg whites until they hold soft peaks. Beat 1-2 tablespoons of egg white into the mixture and then fold in the rest.

Turn into the prepared tin and bake for 35-40 minutes until set. Turn out on to a sheet of greaseproof paper, then carefully peel off the lining paper.

To make the filling, beat together the onion, lemon juice and avocados then beat in the cheese. Season. Spread the filling over the base to within 1 cm/½ inch of the edges. Roll up using the paper as a support. Chill for 1-2 hours.

◼ COOK'S TIP

If the roulade base is not to be served immediately, roll it up round the paper it was turned out on to, and store in the refrigerator up to 24 hours.

177 QUICHE PROVENCALE

Preparation time:
25 minutes, plus chilling

Cooking time:
40-45 minutes

Oven temperature:
190 C, 375 F, gas 5

Makes 1 (20 cm/8 inch) quiche

Total calories: 2,774

YOU WILL NEED:
225 g/8 oz plain flour
pinch of salt
75 g/3 oz butter
25 g/1 oz lard
1 egg yolk
FOR THE FILLING
25 g/1 oz butter
1 onion, sliced
1 garlic clove, crushed
50 g/2 oz button mushrooms, sliced
1 courgette, chopped
2 large tomatoes, chopped
½ teaspoon dried mixed herbs
2 eggs
150 ml/¼ pint single cream
50 g/2 oz Cheddar cheese, grated
25 g/1 oz Gruyère cheese, sliced

Sift the flour and salt into a bowl and rub in the fats. Stir in the egg yolk and enough water to make a firm dough. Turn on to a floured surface and knead lightly. Roll out and line a 20 cm/8 inch flan dish. Chill for 30 minutes, then bake 'blind' in a preheated oven for 15-20 minutes.

Melt the butter in a pan, add the onion and garlic and cook gently for 5 minutes. Add the vegetables and herbs and season well. Cook for 10 minutes. Beat the eggs and cream together and stir in the Cheddar. Spoon the vegetable mixture into the flan case, pour over the egg mixture and arrange the Gruyère slices on top. Bake for 25-30 minutes, until set.

■ COOK'S TIP

This quiche, and the Quiche paysanne (recipe 179) may be served either hot or cold, so can be made well in advance of serving, if liked.

178 COURGETTE FLAN

Preparation time:
25 minutes

Cooking time:
40-50 minutes

Oven temperature:
200 C, 400 F, gas 6, then
160 C, 325 F, gas 3

Makes 1 (25 cm/10 inch) flan

Total calories: 3,192

YOU WILL NEED:
175 g/6 oz plain flour
pinch of salt
75 g/3 oz butter or margarine
2 tablespoons cold water (approximately)
FOR THE FILLING
450 g/1 lb courgettes, sliced
100 g/4 oz Cheddar cheese
300 ml/½ pint single cream
3 eggs, beaten
salt and pepper

Sift the flour and salt into a bowl and rub in the fat until the mixture resembles fine breadcrumbs. Add enough water to mix to a firm dough. Turn on to a floured surface and knead lightly.

Roll out the pastry and use to line a 25 cm/10 inch flan tin. Bake blind in a preheated moderately hot oven for 10 minutes. Remove from the oven and lower the temperature to moderate.

Arrange the courgettes in the flan case. Finely grate the cheese into a bowl. Gradually beat the cream, eggs, and salt and pepper to taste, into the cheese until combined. Pour over the courgettes. Return to the oven and bake for 30-40 minutes, until set. Serve hot or cold.

■ COOK'S TIP

This recipe works well with other vegetables. Try sliced leeks, small broccoli florets (blanched in boiling water for a minute or two), or sliced mushrooms.

179 QUICHE PAYSANNE

Preparation time:
25 minutes, plus chilling

Cooking time:
40-45 minutes

Oven temperature:
190 C, 375 F, gas 5

Makes 1 (20 cm/8 inch) quiche

Total calories: 2,881

YOU WILL NEED:
75 g/3 oz plain flour, sifted
75 g/3 oz wholemeal flour
pinch of salt
75 g/3 oz margarine
4-5 tablespoons iced water
FOR THE FILLING
15 g/1½ oz butter
1 tablespoon oil
4 rashers rindless bacon, chopped
1 large onion, chopped
2 potatoes, sliced
2 eggs
150 ml/¼ pint double cream
1 tablespoon chopped parsley
1 tablespoon chopped chives
½ red pepper, seeded and chopped
75 g/3 oz Cheddar cheese, grated

Make the quiche base as for Quiche provencale (recipe 177), replacing the egg yolk and water with iced water.

Heat the butter and oil in a pan, add the bacon and cook until lightly browned, then drain. Add the onion and potatoes to the pan and cook for 12-15 minutes, until browned. Drain.

Beat the eggs and cream together, stir in the herbs and season well.

Spoon the potatoes, onion and bacon into the flan case and sprinkle over the red pepper. Pour over the egg mixture and sprinkle with the cheese. Return to the oven for 20-25 minutes, until well risen and golden brown.

■ COOK'S TIP

If this quiche, and the Quiche Provencale (recipe 177), are baked in a flan ring set on a baking sheet, rather than in a flan dish or tin, they can easily be transferred to an attractive plate for serving, which would also make them easier to cut.

180 GRANARY LATTICE PIE

Preparation time:
30 minutes, plus chilling

Cooking time:
45 minutes

Oven temperature:
200 C, 400 F, gas 6, then
180 C, 250 F, gas 4

Serves 10

Calories:
359 per portion

YOU WILL NEED:
225 g/8 oz granary flour
100 g/4 oz plain flour
pinch of salt
75 g/3 oz lard
75 g/3 oz margarine
about 5 tablespoons cold water
50 g/2 oz butter
1 onion, finely chopped
450 g/1 lb courgettes, diced
3 eggs
100 g/4 oz Roquefort cheese, crumbled
150 ml/¼ pint milk or single cream

To make the pastry, mix together the flours, add the salt and rub in the fats. Add sufficient water to mix to a pliable dough. Wrap the dough in polythene and chill.

Melt the butter in a pan and add the onion. Fry gently until soft, then add the courgettes and fry until they are lightly browned. Drain.

Whisk the eggs and cheese together, then add the milk or cream and seasoning.

Roll out three-quarters of the pastry and line a 28 cm/11 inch fluted flan ring. Spoon in the courgette mixture then pour the cheese custard over. Roll out the reserved pastry, cut it into strips and lay them over the filling.

Cook in a preheated oven for 25 minutes; reduce the temperature and cook for a further 20-25 minutes until the pie is well risen, golden brown and the pastry cooked. Let cool.

■ COOK'S TIP

This pie may be made the day before it is needed and kept, covered, in the refrigerator. Reheat it before serving in a moderately hot oven.

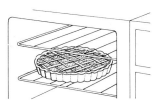

181 WENSLEYDALE FRUIT SALAD

Preparation time:	YOU WILL NEED:
15 minutes	4 red dessert apples
	lemon juice
Serves 12	1 honeydew melon
	2 × 225 g/8 oz cans pineapple slices
Calories:	100 g/4 oz dates, stoned and chopped
192 per portion	4 tablespoons diced cucumber
	4 celery sticks, chopped
	350 g/12 oz Wensleydale cheese, cubed
	300 g/10 oz natural yogurt
	2 teaspoons sugar (optional)
	lettuce, to serve

Core and slice the apples and toss in lemon juice to prevent discoloration. Remove the skin from the melon and discard the seeds. Scoop the flesh into balls, using a melon baller, or cut into dice. Drain the pineapple and cut into bite-size pieces.

Mix together the apple, melon, pineapple, dates, cucumber, celery and cheese in a bowl. Stir in the yogurt and sugar, if using. Toss together well.

Pile the salad into a serving bowl lined with lettuce leaves. Serve immediately.

182 TOMATO AND FETA CHEESE SALAD

Preparation time:	YOU WILL NEED:
10 minutes, plus standing	350 g/12 oz tomatoes, thinly sliced
	1 medium onion, thinly sliced
Serves 4	2 teaspoons chopped fresh oregano or 1 teaspoon dried oregano
Calories:	salt and pepper
241 per portion	100 g/4 oz Feta cheese, crumbled
	4-6 tablespoons olive oil

Arrange the tomato and onion slices in a shallow serving dish. Sprinkle with the oregano, salt and pepper to taste, and the crumbled Feta.

Spoon the olive oil evenly over the top and leave to stand at room temperature for 20 minutes to allow the flavours to mingle.

Serve the salad as a refreshing accompaniment to barbecued meats, such as kebabs.

■ COOK'S TIP

Try other semi-hard cheeses with this recipe, such as Lancashire or Double Gloucester.

■ COOK'S TIP

This is one of the simplest and yet most popular of the Greek salads; occasionally it contains other vegetable ingredients, but this combination has the *'cleanest' and freshest flavour. If preferred, finely shredded fennel can be used instead of tomatoes – the flavour and texture blend well with Feta cheese.*

183 SALADE NICOISE

Preparation time:
15-20 minutes

Serves 4

Calories:
306 per portion

YOU WILL NEED:
1 firm round lettuce
3 firm tomatoes, quartered
2 hard-boiled eggs, quartered
6 anchovy fillets, halved lengthways
12 black olives
2 teaspoons capers
1 × 200 g/7 oz can tuna fish in oil, drained
1 medium red pepper, cored, seeded and cut into strips
6 tablespoons good quality green olive oil
1 large garlic clove, crushed
salt and pepper
1 tablespoon chopped fresh tarragon

Keeping the lettuce whole, wash it well and shake dry. Remove the outer leaves and arrange them around the edge of a salad bowl; cut the remaining lettuce heart into quarters and place in the middle of the bowl.

Add the tomatoes, hard-boiled eggs, anchovy fillets, black olives, capers, tuna fish in chunks, and the strips of red pepper.

Mix the oil with the garlic, salt and pepper to taste, and the chopped tarragon. Spoon the dressing evenly over the salad, and toss lightly before serving.

184 GREEN SALAD

Preparation time:
10 minutes

Serves 8

Calories:
21 per portion

YOU WILL NEED:
1 large head crisp lettuce or 3 lettuce hearts
8 spring onions
½ large cucumber
1 small green pepper
1 head chicory or small bunch watercress or 1 lamb's lettuce
sprig fresh mint
FOR THE DRESSING
150 ml/¼ pint natural yogurt
½ teaspoon made mustard
salt and pepper
pinch of sugar

Wash and trim all of the salad vegetables well in advance and chill.

Near to serving time, assemble the salad in a large bowl. Coarsely shred the lettuce; thinly slice the onions and cucumber; seed and core the pepper and chop coarsely; roughly chop the chicory and mint.

Mix the dressing ingredients together. Spoon over the salad and toss lightly just before serving.

■ COOK'S TIP

This is a very 'earthy' salad, and it should not look too arranged – although Salade Nicoise is colourful to look at and delicious to eat, it should almost look as if it *has been 'thrown together'. The dressing here is basically an oil-based one, but you can add a little lemon juice or wine vinegar, if preferred.*

■ COOK'S TIP

Other ingredients may be used in this salad. Choose ingredients like celery, avocado, curly endive, Chinese cabbage, or finely sliced fennel.

185 WALNUT FLAN

Preparation time:	YOU WILL NEED:
30 minutes	FOR THE PASTRY
	225 g/8 oz plain flour
Cooking time:	pinch of salt
about 1 hour	50 g/2 oz butter or margarine
Oven temperature:	50 g/2 oz lard or white fat
220 C, 425 F, gas 7,	cold water, to mix
then	FOR THE FILLING
190 C, 375 F, gas 5	25 g/1 oz butter or margarine
	175 g/6 oz light soft brown sugar
Serves 10	3 eggs
Calories:	175 ml/6 fl oz maple syrup
414 per portion	1 teaspoon vanilla essence
	grated rind of 1 lemon
	grated rind of ½ orange
	175 g/6 oz walnut halves

To make the pastry, sift the flour and salt into a bowl and rub in the fats until the mixture resembles fine breadcrumbs. Add sufficient water to mix to a pliable dough, then knead lightly.

Roll out the pastry on a lightly floured surface and use to line a 23 cm/9 inch fluted flan ring and bake blind in a pre-heated hot oven for 15 minutes. Reduce the oven temperature.

To make the filling, combine the fat, sugar and eggs in a bowl and beat well; then beat in the maple syrup, vanilla essence and lemon and orange rinds.

Arrange the walnut halves in the pastry case, flat side downwards, and pour the syrup mixture over them.

Bake in the oven for 35-40 minutes. Allow the flan to cool, when the filling will sink back to normal. Serve cold.

■ COOK'S TIP

This is a very rich flan so serve it in small slices. The filling rises rather alarmingly during cooking but sinks back as it cools.

186 EXOTIC MELON COCKTAIL

Preparation time:	YOU WILL NEED:
15 minutes, plus	1 large Ogen melon
chilling	1 large honeydew melon
	450 g/1 lb raspberries, hulled
Serves 10	juice of 3 limes
Calories:	juice of 1 orange
83 per portion	2-3 tablespoons caster sugar (optional)
	1-2 tablespoons finely chopped fresh
	mint

Slice the melons in half, remove the seeds and scoop out the flesh with a melon baller and place it in a serving bowl. Add the raspberries, pour over the fruit juices and stir well to mix. Sweeten with a little sugar, if liked.

Stir in the mint, cover with cling film and chill for 1-2 hours before serving.

■ COOK'S TIP

Other kinds of melon may be used in place of the two suggested here, depending on availability. Be sure to choose melons with contrasting coloured flesh.

187 PEACH AND ALMOND SOUFFLE

Preparation time:
30 minutes, plus
chilling

Serves 6

Calories:
491 per portion

YOU WILL NEED:
6 eggs, separated
100 g/4 oz caster sugar
3 tablespoons Amaretto liqueur
300 ml/½ pint peach purée (see Cook's Tip)
20 g/¾ oz powdered gelatine
3 tablespoons sweet white wine
300 ml/½ pint double or whipping cream
FOR THE DECORATION
3 tablespoons flaked almonds, lightly toasted
2 tablespoons icing sugar

Put the egg yolks into a bowl with the caster sugar and Amaretto liqueur. Whisk until thick, light and creamy. Whisk in the peach purée.

Put the gelatine and wine into a small bowl. Stand the bowl in a pan of hot water and stir until the gelatine has dissolved. Whisk the dissolved gelatine into the peach mixture.

Fix a deep collar of lightly greased, doubled, greaseproof paper around the edge of a lightly greased 900 ml/1½ pint soufflé dish.

Lightly whip the cream and fold gently but thoroughly into the peach mixture. Whisk the egg whites until thick and fold in. Pour into the prepared soufflé dish. Chill until set (about 4 hours).

Sprinkle with the almonds and dust with icing sugar.

■ COOK'S TIP

The peach purée gives the soufflé a much better flavour if it is made from skinned and stoned fresh peaches, but you can use drained canned peaches.

188 CHOCOLATE BRANDY GATEAU

Preparation time:
15 minutes, plus
chilling

Serves 8

Calories:
590 per portion

YOU WILL NEED:
350 g/12 oz plain chocolate, broken into pieces
4 tablespoons strong black coffee
4 tablespoons brandy
225 g/8 oz digestive biscuits, broken into small pieces
175 g/6 oz glacé cherries, quartered
TO FINISH
50 g/2 oz plain chocolate
250 ml/8 fl oz double cream, whipped
few chopped glacé cherry pieces
few angelica pieces

Place the chocolate and coffee in a pan and heat gently until melted; do not allow to become more than lukewarm. Remove from the heat and add the brandy, biscuits and cherries. Mix thoroughly, then turn into a greased 18 cm/7 inch loose-bottomed cake tin. Smooth the top and chill overnight in the refrigerator. Next day, melt the 50 g/2 oz plain chocolate in a bowl over hot water, then spread over the top of the cake. Return to the refrigerator to set.

Remove from the tin and slide on to a plate. Pipe the cream round the top edge of the gateau. Decorate with pieces of glacé cherries and angelica.

■ COOK'S TIP

Instead of melted chocolate, make chocolate caraque: spread a thin layer of melted chocolate on to a marble slab. Leave until firm, but not hard. Draw a *thin-bladed knife at a slight angle across the chocolate with a slight sawing movement, scraping off thin layers in scrolls.*

PARTIES FOR THE YOUNG

Children of all ages will find things to enjoy here. There are amusing snacks to tempt the appetites of small children and hearty dishes to satisfy hungry teenagers.

189 CHIPOLATA KEBABS

Preparation time:
15 minutes

Cooking time:
about 10 minutes

Makes 24

Calories:
73 per portion

YOU WILL NEED:
225 g/8 oz chipolata sausages
1 × 225 g/8 oz can pineapple slices
¼ cucumber, cubed
6 tomatoes, quartered
225 g/8 oz Cheddar cheese, cubed
12 stoned dates, halved
1 grapefruit

Grill the chipolatas, turning frequently, until cooked. Cool and cut into 2.5 cm/1 inch pieces.

Drain and chop the pineapple slices. Thread pieces of sausage, pineapple, cucumber, tomato, cheese and date on to cocktail sticks.

Cut a slice from the grapefruit to enable it to stand, cut side down. Stick the small kebabs into the grapefruit.

190 CELERY BOATS

Preparation time:
20 minutes

Makes about 20

Calories:
26 per portion

YOU WILL NEED:
100 g/4 oz cream cheese
1 tablespoon chopped chives (see Cook's Tip)
salt and pepper
1 head of celery, divided into sticks
TO FINISH:
rice paper
cocktail sticks
few lettuce leaves, shredded

Place the cheese in a bowl with the chives and salt and pepper to taste. Mix well until smooth. Spoon a little of the mixture into each celery stick and spread smoothly. Cut into 6 cm/2½ inch lengths.

Cut the rice paper into triangles, spear with a cocktail stick and stick into the celery.

Arrange the lettuce on a serving dish and place the celery boats on top.

■ COOK'S TIP

If these kebabs are made well in advance of the party, keep them fresh by putting them, stuck into the grapefruit, in a plastic food bag in the refrigerator.

■ COOK'S TIP

Use kitchen scissors rather than a chopping knife to snip chives into tiny pieces: it is quicker and the chives do not get bruised or squashed.

191 PINWHEEL SANDWICHES

Preparation time:
15 minutes

Makes about 32

Calories:
63 per portion

YOU WILL NEED:
4 slices medium sliced brown bread,
*   crusts removed*
FOR THE FILLING
75 g/3 oz cream cheese
1 tablespoon mayonnaise
salt and pepper
1 celery stick

For the filling, beat the cream cheese with the mayonnaise and salt and pepper to taste. Cut the celery into four 5 mm/¼ inch sticks, the same length as the bread. Roll out the bread lightly with a rolling pin and spread thickly with the cheese filling. Place a stick of celery across one end of each slice. Roll up tightly, pressing the edge down firmly.

Cut the rolls into 1 cm/½ inch slices to serve.

192 CHESSBOARD SANDWICHES

Preparation time:
25 minutes

Makes 32

Calories:
93 per portion

YOU WILL NEED:
8 slices brown bread
8 slices white bread
FOR THE FILLINGS
50 g/2 oz butter
6 tablespoons mayonnaise
3 hard-boiled eggs, finely chopped (see
*   Cook's Tip)*
50 g/2 oz cream cheese
75 g/3 oz Cheddar cheese, grated
2 tablespoons chopped chives
salt and pepper

For the fillings, beat the butter with the mayonnaise; divide in half. Stir the chopped eggs into one portion; mix the cheeses and chives into the other portion. Season both with salt and pepper to taste.

Make the sandwiches using one slice of brown bread, one slice of white and one filling for each. Remove the crusts, then cut each sandwich into four squares.

Arrange them in two layers on a square cake board, alternating the brown and white sides to create a chessboard effect.

■ COOK'S TIP

Wrap the completed bread rolls in cling film and keep them whole in the refrigerator until required. Do not wrap them with other sandwiches or rolls
containing stronger-flavoured fillings as the cream cheese filling could absorb the strong flavours.

■ COOK'S TIP

To prevent the edges of the yolks of hard-boiled eggs turning black, put the cooked eggs, still in their shells, straight into cold water until they are cold.

193 PIZZA NAPOLETANA

Preparation time:
25 minutes, plus
rising and proving

Cooking time:
35-40 minutes

Oven temperature:
220 C, 425 F, gas 7

Serves 8

Calories:
199 per portion

YOU WILL NEED:
330 g/10 oz strong white plain flour
salt and pepper
1 teaspoon dried yeast
1 teaspoon caster sugar
250 ml/8 fl oz warm water (approx)
1 tablespoon oil
1 onion, chopped
1 garlic clove, crushed
1 × 397 g/14 oz can tomatoes
2 tablespoons dry white wine
½ teaspoon each dried oregano and
    basil
1 tablespoon tomato purée
100 g/4 oz Mozzarella cheese, diced

For the pizza dough, sift the flour and a pinch of salt into a bowl. Mix the yeast with the sugar and 2 tablespoons of the water and leave for 10 minutes, then add to the flour with enough water to give a firm dough. Knead on a floured surface for about 15 minutes, until the dough is elastic. Cover and leave in a warm place until doubled in size. Press the dough into the base and sides of a 23 cm/9 inch loose-bottomed tin.

For the tomato sauce, heat the oil in a pan, add the onion and garlic and cook for 2-3 minutes, until translucent. Add the tomatoes with their juices, the wine, herbs, and salt and pepper to taste. Bring to the boil and cook rapidly for 12-15 minutes, until thickened. Stir in the tomato purée.

Spread evenly over the dough and arrange the cheese on top. Bake in a preheated oven for 20 minutes.

194 LITTLE PIZZAS

Preparation time:
25 minutes, plus
rising and proving

Cooking time:
30-40 minutes

Serves 4-6

Calories:
537-358 per portion

YOU WILL NEED:
1 quantity pizza dough (see recipe
    193)
1 quantity tomato sauce (see recipe
    193)
FOR THE TOPPING
100 g/4 oz Mozzarella cheese, diced
1 tablespoon grated Parmesan cheese
100 g/4 oz Italian Mortadella or
    salami, chopped
1-2 garlic cloves, crushed

Prepare the pizza dough and tomato sauce as for Pizza Napoletana (recipe 193). When the dough has risen, knead it again and divide into 8 or 12 pieces. Form each into a round.

Heat a little oil in a large frying pan and fry 2 or 3 rounds at a time for about 5-7 minutes, until golden brown on each side.

Spread the hot sauce on the pizzas and top with the cheeses, Mortadella or salami and garlic. Return to the pan and cook for 3 minutes. Fold in half and serve immediately.

◼ COOK'S TIP

A hard English cheese, such as Cheddar or Cheshire, may be used on top of the pizza, instead of Mozzarella, if preferred.

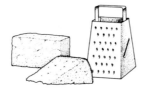

◼ COOK'S TIP

Vary these pizzas by adding different toppings. Chopped cooked ham, slices of cooked sausage, or chunks of canned tuna would appeal to young people.

195 POTATO CRISP COOKIES

Preparation time:
20 minutes

Cooking time:
15 minutes

Oven temperature:
190 C, 375 F, gas 5

Makes 10

Calories:
124 per portion

YOU WILL NEED:
90 g/3½ oz Gruyère cheese, grated
2 × 25 g/1 oz packets cheese-and
    onion-flavoured potato crisps,
    lightly crushed
2 teaspoons sesame seeds
65 g/2½ oz plain flour
¾ teaspoon dry mustard
good pinch of garlic powder
pinch of cayenne pepper
65 g/2½ oz butter or margarine,
    melted

Put the cheese into a bowl and mix in the crushed crisps, sesame seeds, flour, mustard, garlic powder and cayenne. Add the butter and mix lightly to form a dough.

Divide the mixture into 10 even-sized pieces and put them in rough heaps on a greased baking sheet.

Bake in a preheated oven for about 15 minutes until lightly browned. If the cheese spreads during cooking, mould it back into shape with a small palette knife.

Cool the cookies on the baking sheet for 3-4 minutes, then carefully remove them to a wire rack.

196 TURKEY BITES WITH TOMATO DIP

Preparation time:
20 minutes

Cooking time:
20 minutes

Serves 12

Calories:
84 per portion

YOU WILL NEED:
3 turkey breast fillets, total weight
    about 450 g/1 lb
little seasoned flour
1 egg, beaten
about 100 g/4 oz fresh white
    breadcrumbs or 1 packet golden
    breadcrumbs
deep oil or fat for frying
FOR THE TOMATO DIP
4 tablespoons chunky tomato pickle
4 tablespoons tomato ketchup
2 tablespoons soured cream

Cut the turkey fillets into narrow strips about 5 × 1.5 cm/2 × ½ inch. Toss them in seasoned flour, then dip in beaten egg and coat thoroughly with the breadcrumbs.

Heat the deep fat to 180-190 C/350-375 F or until a cube of bread browns in 30 seconds. Fry the turkey pieces, a few at a time, for 3-4 minutes until they are golden brown and crisp. Drain on absorbent kitchen paper. Keep the first batch warm while frying the rest.

Combine all the ingredients for the dip and put them into a small serving bowl.

Serve the turkey on a plate with the bowl of tomato dip.

■ COOK'S TIP

These cookies should be eaten the day they are made and are at their best if served warm. Do not be tempted to freeze them.

■ COOK'S TIP

Since these turkey bites are equally good served hot or cold, they and the dip may be prepared in advance. Keep the dip covered until required.

197 CHEESE AND ONION QUICHE

Preparation time:
20 minutes

Cooking time:
40-45 minutes

Oven temperature:
190 C, 375 F, gas 5

Makes 3 × 23 cm/ 9 inch quiches

Calories:
1,584 per quiche

YOU WILL NEED:
450 g/1 lb plain flour
½ teaspoon salt
1 teaspoon dry mustard
225 g/8 oz butter or margarine
225 g/8 oz Cheddar cheese, grated
6 tablespoons water (approximately)
FOR THE FILLING
6 tablespoons oil
6 onions, chopped
9 eggs
600 ml/1 pint milk
750 g/1½ lb Cheddar cheese, grated
3 tablespoons chopped parsley
salt and pepper

To make the cheese pastry for the base, sift the flour, salt and mustard into a bowl. Rub in the fat until the mixture resembles breadcrumbs, then stir in the cheese. Add the water gradually and mix to a firm dough. Turn on to a floured surface and knead lightly.

Divide the dough into 3 pieces, roll out and use to line three 23 cm/9 inch flan tins. Chill for 15 minutes.

Meanwhile, make the filling. Heat the oil in a pan, add the onions and fry gently until transparent. Beat the eggs and milk together in a large bowl, then stir in the cheese, onions, parsley, and salt and pepper to taste.

Divide between the pastry cases and bake in a preheated oven for 35-40 minutes, until set. Serve hot or cold.

■ COOK'S TIP

The pastry cases may be baked blind in advance. Put foil into each one, and put baking beans (or a dry pulse) on top to prevent the pastry rising up as it cooks.

Use the same oven temperature as in the main recipe.

198 SURPRISE SAUSAGE ROLLS

Preparation time:
15 minutes

Cooking time:
20-25 minutes

Oven temperature:
200 C, 400 F, gas 6

Makes 16

Calories:
184 per portion

YOU WILL NEED:
450 g/1 lb chipolata sausages
4 tablespoons peanut butter
1 tablespoon French mustard
2-3 tablespoons water
16 thin slices brown bread, crusts removed
50 g/2 oz soft margarine

Grill the sausages under a preheated hot grill, turning frequently, until browned all over. Put the peanut butter and mustard in a bowl, add the water and mix thoroughly. Roll the bread lightly with a rolling pin, then spread with the peanut mixture.

Place a sausage diagonally across each slice of bread and roll up tightly, securing with a cocktail stick. Spread each roll with margarine and place on a baking sheet. Bake in a preheated oven for 15-20 minutes, until golden.

■ COOK'S TIP

Butter may be used instead of peanut butter, in which case omit the water.

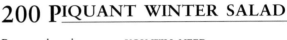

199 FRANKFURTER AND BACON ROLLS

Preparation time:
15 minutes

Cooking time:
5 minutes

Makes 14

Calories:
130 per roll

YOU WILL NEED:
14 *frankfurters*
4 *processed cheese slices*
14 *rashers rindless streaky bacon*
14 *bridge rolls, split open*

Make a cut along each frankfurter, two-thirds of the way through. Cut each slice of cheese into 4 strips and place one in each frankfurter.

Stretch the bacon with a palette knife and wind one rasher around each frankfurter to cover the cheese.

Cook under a preheated hot grill for 5 minutes, turning occasionally.

Place a frankfurter inside each roll.

200 PIQUANT WINTER SALAD

Preparation time:
20 minutes

Cooking time:
about 15 minutes

Serves 4

Calories:
421 per portion

YOU WILL NEED:
450 g/1 lb small waxy potatoes
1 small onion, chopped
2 celery sticks, chopped
2 carrots, grated
2 heads chicory
100 g/4 oz ham
50 g/2 oz salami
salt and pepper
FOR THE DRESSING
150 ml/¼ pint soured cream
2 tablespoons mayonnaise
2 tablespoons chopped chives
1 teaspoon mustard
2 tablespoons green peppercorns
1 tablespoon chopped parsley
3 hard-boiled eggs

Cook the potatoes in their skins until tender. Drain, then remove the skins. Slice the potatoes and place in a salad bowl with the onion, celery and carrots. Reserve a few chicory leaves for garnish. Slice the remaining chicory and ham; dice the salami. Add to the bowl with salt and pepper to taste. Toss well.

To make the dressing, mix all the ingredients except the hard-boiled eggs together and season with salt and pepper. Cut the eggs in half and separate the whites from the yolks. Chop the whites and add to the dressing. Spoon over the salad and toss lightly. Sieve the egg yolks and sprinkle over the salad. Garnish with the chicory leaves.

■ COOK'S TIP

*Most children will probably
be happiest eating these
rolls with tomato ketchup,
but a vegetable relish would
make an unusual
alternative.*

■ COOK'S TIP

*If soured cream is not
available, use ordinary
double or whipping cream
and add one teaspoon of
lemon juice to the dressing.*

201 CHICKEN A LA KING

Preparation time:
15 minutes

Cooking time:
about 20 minutes

Serves 20

Calories:
161 per portion

YOU WILL NEED:
150 ml/¼ pint oil
4 onions, chopped
3 green peppers, cored, seeded and diced
750 g/1½ lb button mushrooms, quartered
100 g/4 oz plain flour
300 ml/½ pint milk
1.2 litres/2 pints chicken stock
1.5 kg/3 lb cooked chicken, diced
1 teaspoon paprika
salt
150 ml/¼ pint single cream
1 tablespoon lemon juice

Heat the oil in a large pan, add the onions and diced peppers and fry until softened. Add the mushrooms and cook stirring for 2 minutes. Stir in the flour and cook for 1 minute, then gradually stir in the milk. Bring to the boil, stirring.

Add the stock and simmer for 3 minutes, until thickened. Add the chicken, paprika and salt to taste. Simmer for 5 minutes until heated through.

Remove from the heat and stir in the cream and lemon juice. Serve with plain boiled rice.

202 BARBECUED SPARE RIBS

Preparation time:
10 minutes, plus marinating

Cooking time:
5-10 minutes

Serves 12

Calories:
421 per portion

YOU WILL NEED:
2 kg/4½ lb pork spare ribs
FOR THE MARINADE
2 teaspoons soy sauce
2 teaspoons Worcestershire sauce
4 tablespoons tomato ketchup
2 tablespoons fruit sauce
2 teaspoons soft brown sugar
1 teaspoon French mustard

Mix the marinade ingredients together in a small basin. Cut the ribs into serving pieces and brush with the marinade. Leave to marinate for 1-2 hours, reserving any left-over marinade.

Place the ribs on the barbecue grid and cook for 5-10 minutes, turning frequently and basting with the remaining marinade until crisp.

Serve the spare ribs with a chunky sauce, such as Sweet and sour sauce (recipe 203).

■ COOK'S TIP

About 750 g/1½ lb of rice should be served with this quantity of chicken. The rice can be cooked before the chicken and kept warm in buttered foil in a
moderate oven (160 C, 325 F, gas 3) for 30 minutes. Cooked turkey could replace the chicken in the main recipe.

■ COOK'S TIP

These spare ribs can be cooked under a grill. Line the bottom of the grill pan with foil to prevent the marinade burning on to it.

203 SWEET AND SOUR SAUCE

Preparation time:
10 minutes

Cooking time:
25-30 minutes

Makes about
450 ml/¾ pint

Total calories: 592

YOU WILL NEED:
2 small onions
2 small carrots
2 tablespoons oil
1 × 225 g/8 oz can pineapple pieces
6 tablespoons malt vinegar
1 tablespoon Worcestershire sauce
1 tablespoon soy sauce
5 tablespoons clear honey
4 teaspoons cornflour
6 tablespoons water
salt and pepper

Chop the onions and carrots finely. Heat the oil in a pan, add the onions and carrots and fry for 5 minutes, until softened. Pour the pineapple juice into the pan. Add the vinegar, sauces and honey and simmer for 15 minutes, stirring occasionally.

Blend the cornflour with the water and stir into the sauce.

Add the pineapple, and salt and pepper to taste. Bring to the boil, stirring, then simmer for about 5 minutes until thickened.

204 MOUSSAKA

Preparation time:
20 minutes

Cooking time:
about 1 hour 15 minutes

Serves 20

Calories:
354 per portion

YOU WILL NEED:
1.5 kg/3 lb aubergines, sliced
salt and pepper
300 ml/½ pint vegetable oil
6 onions, chopped
1.5 kg/3 lb lamb, minced
3 garlic cloves, crushed
3 tablespoons tomato purée
3 × 397 g/14 oz cans tomatoes
1.5 kg/3 lb potatoes, parboiled
75 g/3 oz butter or margarine
75 g/3 oz plain flour
900 ml/1½ pints milk
3 egg yolks
100 g/4 oz Cheddar cheese, grated

Heat some of the oil in 2 large frying pans and fry the aubergine slices in batches until golden. Set aside.

Add a little more oil to the pans, and fry the onions until soft. Add the meat and garlic and fry briskly, stirring, for 10 minutes. Drain off excess fat. Add 1 teaspoon salt, and pepper to taste, to each pan. Stir in the tomato purée and tomatoes, with their juice. Bring to the boil and simmer for 30 minutes.

Layer the aubergines, meat mixture and thickly sliced potatoes in 3 casseroles, finishing with aubergines.

To make the sauce topping, melt the fat in a pan and stir in the flour. Gradually stir in the milk and cook, stirring, until thickened. Remove from the heat and stir in the egg yolks, and salt and pepper to taste. Pour over the aubergines and sprinkle with cheese. Bake in a preheated oven for 15 minutes.

■ COOK'S TIP

This sauce is very good with barbecued or grilled chicken drumsticks, spare ribs (see recipe 202), and even sausages.

■ COOK'S TIP

To draw the harsh-tasting juice from aubergines, sprinkle the slices with salt and leave for 30 minutes. Drain off the juices and dry the slices.

205 CHINESE CABBAGE SALAD

Preparation time:
15 minutes

Serves 20

Calories:
91 per portion

YOU WILL NEED:
2 small Chinese cabbages, shredded
450 g/1 lb bean sprouts
2 bunches watercress
1 apple, sliced
2 avocados
FOR THE DRESSING
150 ml/¼ pint olive oil
4 tablespoons wine vinegar
1 teaspoon sugar
1 teaspoon French mustard
2 tablespoons chopped mixed herbs
(mint, parsley, chives, thyme)

Place the cabbage and bean sprouts in a salad bowl. Separate the watercress into sprigs; add to the bowl with the apple slices.

Place the dressing ingredients in a screw-topped jar and shake well. Peel the avocados and slice them into another bowl. Pour over the dressing to coat. Add to the remaining salad and toss well before serving.

206 TOFFEE APPLES

Preparation time:
15 minutes

Cooking time:
20 minutes

Serves 6

Calories:
225 per portion

YOU WILL NEED:
6 eating apples, washed, dried and
stalks removed
6 wooden sticks
175 g/6 oz sugar
25 g/1 oz butter
50 g/2 oz golden syrup
½ teaspoon lemon juice
6 tablespoons water

Push a wooden stick into each apple.

Place the sugar, butter, golden syrup, lemon juice and water in a heavy-based pan. Stir gently over a low heat until the sugar has dissolved, then increase the heat and boil rapidly until the toffee registers 145 C/290 F on the sugar thermometer.

Dip the apples into the pan one at a time, twisting the pan to coat evenly.

Immediately plunge each apple into a bowl of cold water to set the toffee, then stand them on a piece of oiled grease-proof paper until cold.

■ COOK'S TIP

The type of Chinese cabbage most commonly sold in the UK looks similar to a cos lettuce. Its Chinese name is Pe-tsai. Another Chinese cabbage, Pak-choi is more like spinach or chard. It is also good in salads.

■ COOK'S TIP

If you do not have a sugar thrmometer, test if the syrup is hot enough by dropping a spoonful into cold water: it should form brittle threads which snap.

207 BANANA ICE CREAM

Preparation time:
15 minutes, plus
cooling and freezing

Cooking time:
about 10 minutes

Serves 20

Calories:
176 per portion

YOU WILL NEED:
450 ml/3/4 pint milk
175 g/6 oz caster sugar
3 eggs, beaten
1 teaspoon vanilla essence
450 ml/3/4 pint double cream
6 bananas, mashed

Put the milk, sugar and eggs in a small pan and heat gently, stirring constantly, until the mixture thickens. Strain into a bowl and add the vanilla essence. Leave to cool.

Whip the cream until slightly thickened and fold into the cooled custard. Stir in the mashed bananas. Pour into a rigid freezerproof container, cover, seal and freeze until firm.

Transfer to the refrigerator about 1 hour before serving to soften.

208 MARSHMALLOW CORNETS

Preparation time:
20 minutes, plus
freezing

Cooking time:
about 15 minutes

Makes 12

Calories:
321 per cornet

YOU WILL NEED:
3 egg yolks
75 g/3 oz soft brown sugar
175 g/6 oz plain chocolate, chopped
300 ml/1/2 pint single cream
150 ml/1/4 pint double cream
*100 g/4 oz marshamallows, each
    snipped into four pieces*
*50 g/2 oz split almonds, browned and
    chopped*
12 ice cream cornets

Beat the egg yolks with the sugar in a heatproof bowl until creamy. Place the chocolate in a pan with the single cream and heat gently until melted. Bring just to the boil, then pour on to the egg yolk mixture thoroughly. Place the bowl over a pan of simmering water and stir constantly until thickened. Strain and allow to cool.

Whip the double cream until it forms soft peaks, then fold in the chocolate custard. Pour into a rigid freezerproof container, cover and freeze for 2-3 hours until half-frozen. Stir well, then mix in the marshmallows and almonds. Return to the freezer and freeze until firm.

Serve in ice cream cornets.

■ COOK'S TIP

If the ice cream is to be served as part of a buffet, either leave it in its freezer container, wrapped in a pretty cloth, or transfer it to a well-chilled dish.

■ COOK'S TIP

Transfer the frozen ice cream mixture to the refrigerator 20 minutes before it is to be served, to allow it to soften sufficiently to be scooped into cornets.

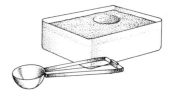

209 CHOCOLATE PEANUT BARS

Preparation time:
10 minutes

Cooking time: 6-8 minutes

Makes 20

Calories:
104 per biscuit

YOU WILL NEED:
100 g/4 oz plain chocolate, chopped
75 g/3 oz crunchy peanut butter
4 tablespoons golden syrup
1 tablespoon water
75 g/3 oz unsalted peanuts, chopped
100 g/4 oz bran flakes

Place the chocolate, peanut butter, syrup and water in a pan and heat gently until melted. Stir in the peanuts and bran flakes and mix thoroughly.

Turn into a lined and greased 18 × 28 cm/7 × 11 inch baking tin and smooth the surface. Chill in the refrigerator until set. Cut into bars to serve.

210 GINGERBREAD PEOPLE

Preparation time:
25 minutes, plus cooling and chilling

Cooking time:
10-15 minutes

Oven temperature:
160 C, 325 F, gas 3

Makes 12

Calories:
117 per biscuit

YOU WILL NEED:
100 g/4 oz plain flour
½ teaspoon bicarbonate of soda
½ teaspoon ground ginger
½ teaspoon ground cinnamon
25 g/1 oz butter or margarine
50 g/2 oz soft brown sugar
2 tablespoons golden syrup
1 teaspoon milk
FOR THE DECORATION
currants
glacé cherries

Sift the flour, soda and spices into a bowl. Place the fat, sugar and syrup in a pan over low heat until melted. Cool, then mix into the flour with the milk to make a firm dough. Wrap in polythene and chill for 30 minutes.

Turn the dough on to a floured surface and roll out to a 5mm/¼ inch thickness. Using gingerbread cutters, cut out 12 figures. Press on currants for buttons and eyes and pieces of glacé cherry for mouths. Place on greased baking sheets.

Bake in a preheated oven for 10-15 minutes, until firm. Transfer to a wire rack to cool.

■ COOK'S TIP

For a refreshing lemonade to serve with many of the recipes in this chapter, finely grate the rind of 4 lemons and put in a heatproof jug with 75 g/3 oz sugar. Pour
over 1.2 litres/2 pints boiling water and stir to dissolve the sugar. Add the juice from the lemons. Cool, strain into a jug and chill until required.

■ COOK'S TIP

White glacé icing (see recipe 211) piped through a fine nozzle, may be used instead of the fruit to decorate the biscuits. Add it when the cooked biscuits are cold.

211 SMARTIE BUNS

Preparation time:
20 minutes, plus chilling

Cooking time:
15 minutes

Oven temperature:
180 C, 350 F, gas 4

Makes 24

Calories:
57 per bun

YOU WILL NEED:
50 g/2 oz soft margarine
50 g/2 oz self-raising flour, sifted
pinch of baking powder
1 egg
FOR THE TOPPING
50 g/2 oz glacé icing (see Cook's Tip)
selection of food colourings
24 Smarties

Place the cake ingredients in a mixing bowl and beat vigorously until thoroughly blended.

Arrange 24 petits fours cases on a baking sheet and fill each one two-thirds full with mixture. Bake in a preheated oven for 15 minutes. Cool on a wire rack.

Divide the icing into several portions and colour each one with a few drops of colouring. Spoon a little icing on to the centre of each cake and top with a Smartie.

212 TRAFFIC LIGHT BISCUITS

Preparation time:
20-25 minutes

Cooking time:
15-20 minutes

Oven temperature:
160 C, 325 F, gas 3

Makes 9

Calories:
147 per biscuit

YOU WILL NEED:
25 g/1 oz caster sugar
50 g/2 oz butter or margarine
75 g/3 oz plain flour, sifted
FOR THE TOPPING
50 g/2 oz glacé icing (see Cook's Tip, recipe 211)
few drops each of red, yellow and green food colouring
1 tablespoon red jam

Beat the sugar and fat together until light and fluffy. Add the flour and mix until the mixture blends together.

Turn on to a floured surface and knead until smooth. Roll out to an oblong 4mm/³/₁₆ inch thick and cut into 2.5 × 7.5 cm/1 × 3 inch strips. Cut out 3 circles with a 1.5 cm/³/₄ inch pastry cutter or piping nozzle from each of half the strips.

Place all the strips on baking sheets and bake in a preheated oven for 15-20 minutes, until pale golden. Leave to cool on the baking sheets.

Divide the icing into 3 portions and colour each with a food colouring (red, yellow and green). Spread the plain biscuits with a thin layer of jam. Place the biscuits with holes in on top. Fill the holes with the coloured icing to represent the traffic lights.

■ COOK'S TIP

To make glacé icing, gradually stir 1 tablespoon warm water into 100 g/4 oz sifted icing sugar. The icing should be thick enough to coat the back of the spoon thickly. Only a few drops of food colouring will be necessary.

■ COOK'S TIP

For a quick alternative to coloured glacé icing, fill the holes in the biscuits with halves of red, yellow and green glacé cherries.

Coffee and Tea Parties

Coffee parties are a good way to welcome newcomers to the neighbourhood – and of fundraising. Just offer a choice of homemade delights from this chapter!

213 Cassata Alla Siciliana

Preparation time:
40 minutes plus chilling

Serves 6

Calories:
1,088 per portion

YOU WILL NEED:
350 g/12 oz ricotta cheese, sieved
100 g/4 oz caster sugar
25 g/1 oz vanilla sugar (see recipe 220)
150 ml/¼ pint double cream, whipped
175 g/6 oz crystallized fruit, chopped
25 g/1 oz shelled pistachio nuts, chopped
3 × 18 cm/7 inch sponge layers
4 tablespoons Strega
1 tablespoon chocolate coffee beans
FOR THE ICING
175 g/6 oz butter, softened
275 g/10 oz icing sugar, sifted
100 g/4 oz plain chocolate, melted
3 tablespoons cold strong black coffee

Combine the cheese and the sugars. Beat the cream into the cheese mixture, then stir in the fruit and nuts. Sprinkle each sponge layer with the Strega. Put one layer into a deep 18 cm/7 inch cake tin. Cover with half the cheese mixture, then insert a second layer. Cover with the remaining cheese mixture, and top with the remaining sponge layer. Lay a plate on top and add a 450 g/1 lb weight. Chill overnight.

Beat the icing ingredients together. Chill for 2 hours.

Turn the cake on to a serving plate. Swirl the icing over the top and sides. Decorate with the chocolate beans.

214 Flapjacks

Preparation time:
10 minutes

Cooking time:
25-30 minutes

Oven temperature:
180 C, 350 F, gas 4

Makes 16

Calories:
154 per flapjack

YOU WILL NEED:
100 g/4 oz margarine
100 g/4 oz soft brown sugar
75 g/3 oz golden syrup
225 g/8 oz rolled oats

Melt the margarine with the sugar and syrup, then stir in the rolled oats and mix thoroughly. Turn into a greased, shallow 20 cm/8 inch square tin. and smooth the top with a palette knife.

Bake in a preheated oven for 25-30 minutes until golden brown.

Cool in the tin for 2 minutes, then cut into fingers. Cool completely before removing from the tin.

■ COOK'S TIP

If ricotta cheese is unavailable, replace with drained cottage cheese. Whipping cream can be used instead of double cream (to reduce the calories) and chopped mixed peel substituted for the crystallized fruit.

■ COOK'S TIP

If rolled oats are stored in airtight containers in a cool place they keep well for several months. They are an important source of protein and fibre in the diet.

215 HIGH BUTTER SHORTIES

Preparation time:
25 minutes, plus
cooling

Cooking time:
10-12 minutes

Oven temperature:
190 C, 375 F, gas 5

Makes about 26

Calories:
119 per biscuit

YOU WILL NEED:
225 g/8 oz butter, softened
50 g/2 oz caster sugar
½ teaspoon vanilla essence
225 g/8 oz plain flour, sifted
7 blanched almonds
3 glacé cherries, halved
50 g/2 oz plain chocolate, broken into
*   pieces*

Cream the softened butter and sugar with a wooden spoon until light and fluffy. Mix in the vanilla essence and the flour to form a soft mixture. Place the mixture in a piping bag fitted with a large star nozzle and pipe thirteen 7.5 cm/3 inch finger lengths on to a greased baking tray. Bake in a preheated oven for 10 minutes, until pale golden. Transfer to a wire rack and leave to cool completely.

Meanwhile, pipe the remaining mixture into 13 stars on a greased baking tray. Top 7 of these with a blanched almond and the remaining stars with a halved glacé cherry. Bake for 12 minutes, until pale golden and cooked through. Transfer to a wire rack and leave to cool completely.

Place the chocolate pieces in a heatproof basin over a saucepan of hot but not boiling water until melted (do not stir the chocolate). Dip the ends of the finger biscuits in the melted chocolate and leave to set for about 45 minutes on a wire rack.

216 DROP SCONES

Preparation time:
10 minutes

Cooking time:
about 12 minutes

Makes 16

Calories:
74 per scone

YOU WILL NEED:
225 g/8 oz plain flour
1 teaspoon cream of tartar
½ teaspoon bicarbonate of soda
½ teaspoon salt
25 g/1 oz sugar
1 large egg
150 ml/8 fl oz milk
1 tablespoon oil

Sift the dry ingredients together into a mixing bowl and make a well in the centre. Add the egg and half the milk and mix to a smooth batter. Gradually beat in the remaining milk with the oil, mixing to a thick batter.

Heat a heavy frying pan or griddle and grease lightly. Drop tablespoonfuls of the batter on to the griddle and cook until the top is blistered. Turn with a palette knife and cook until the underside is golden brown. Place the scones inside a clean folded tea-towel to keep moist until they are all cooked. Serve with butter.

■ COOK'S TIP

When baking large quantities of biscuits, sets of folding wire racks are invaluable as space-savers. The racks can be placed on top of each other.

■ COOK'S TIP

Traditionally griddles were made of cast-iron, sometimes with a semi-circular handle. They are also known as girdles and bakestones. After use just *rub with absorbent kitchen paper moistened with a little oil.*

217 ALMOND GALETTES

Preparation time:
25 minutes

Cooking time:
15-20 minutes

Oven temperature:
180 C, 350 F, gas 4

Makes 24

Calories:
103 per galette

YOU WILL NEED:
100 g/4 oz butter or margarine
50 g/2 oz caster sugar
1 egg yolk
50 g/2 oz ground almonds
175 g/6 oz plain flour
FOR THE TOPPING
100 g/4 oz icing sugar, sifted
1 egg white
50 g/2 oz flaked almonds

Cream the butter and margarine and sugar together, then add the egg yolk and beat well. Add the ground almonds and flour and mix well. Knead lightly and roll out thinly. Cut into rounds using a 6 cm/2½ inch plain cutter and place on a greased baking tray.

For the topping, mix the icing sugar with the egg white, then add the flaked almonds and stir well. Spoon over the biscuits and bake in a preheated oven for 15-20 minutes until golden brown. Cool on a baking tray.

218 PANDOLCE

Preparation time:
25 minutes, plus proving

Cooking time:
50-55 minutes

Oven temperature:
220 C, 425 F, gas 7

Serves 8

Calories:
494 per portion

YOU WILL NEED:
20 g/¾ oz fresh yeast or 3 teaspoons dried yeast
100 g/4 oz caster sugar
4 tablespoons tepid water
450 g/1 lb plain flour
75 g/3 oz butter, melted
1 egg, beaten
225 g/8 oz crystallized fruits, chopped or chopped mixed peel
75 g/3 oz blanched almonds, chopped

Crumble the yeast into a small bowl. Cream with 1 teaspoon of the sugar, and mix in the tepid water. Leave in a warm place to froth – about 10 minutes. Sift the flour into a bowl and make a well in the centre; add the yeast liquid, the remaining sugar, the melted butter and beaten egg. Work to a smooth dough. Put the dough into a floured bowl and cover with a damp tea-towel or large freezer bag. Leave in a warm place for 1 hour or until doubled in bulk.

Knock back the dough and knead in the chopped fruits and almonds. Shape the dough into a large round loaf and place on a greased baking tray or into an 18 cm/7 inch greased brioche tin. Cover again and leave for 40-45 minutes or until doubled in bulk. Bake in a preheated oven for 50-55 minutes, covering with foil once the top of the loaf has browned well. Cool on a wire rack.

◼ COOK'S TIP

Remove the butter, if using, from the refrigerator in advance so that it reaches room temperature before you start cooking. It is then easier to cream.

◼ COOK'S TIP

Fresh yeast is usually available from health food shops and also some bakers. Keep the yeast carefully wrapped to prevent it drying out. Store in the *refrigerator. Test with a fine skewer to see that the bread is cooked through, if the skewer does not come out clean, bake the bread for about 10 minutes longer.*

219 OAT CRUNCHIES

Preparation time:
15 minutes, plus
standing

Cooking time:
15-20 minutes

Oven temperature:
160 C, 325 F, gas 3

Makes 30

Calories:
78 per biscuit

YOU WILL NEED: 、
100 g/4 oz rolled oats
50 g/2 oz medium oatmeal
150 g/5 oz soft brown sugar
120 ml/4 fl oz vegetable oil
1 egg
½ teaspoon almond essence

Place the oats, oatmeal, sugar and oil in a bowl, mix well and leave to stand for 1 hour. Add the egg and almond essence and beat together thoroughly. Place teaspoonfuls of the mixture well apart on a greased baking tray and press flat with a damp fork.

Bake in a preheated oven for 15-20 minutes until golden brown. Leave to cool for 2 minutes, then transfer to a wire rack to cool completely.

---

220 QUESADILLAS

Preparation time:
40 minutes, plus
chilling

Cooking time:
20-25 minutes

Oven temperature:
200 C, 400 F, gas 6

Makes 10

Calories:
329 per portion

YOU WILL NEED:
FOR THE PASTRY
350 g/12 oz plain flour
generous pinch of salt
½ teaspoon mixed spice
175 g/6 oz butter
1 egg, beaten
1 egg yolk
4 tablespoons water
milk, for glazing
vanilla sugar (see Cook's Tip)
FOR THE FILLING
225 g/8 oz cottage cheese, drained
½ teaspoon mixed spice
1 egg
2 egg yolks
50 g/2 oz currants
50 g/2 oz flaked almonds

Sift the flour, salt and mixed spice into a bowl. Rub in the butter. Mix the egg with the egg yolk and water. Stir into the dry ingredients and work into a smooth dough. Shape into a ball, wrap in cling film and chill for 30 minutes.

To make the filling, combine the ingredients.

Roll out half of the pastry and line the base of a greased, shallow tin, 28 × 18 cm/11 × 7 inch. Spread the filling over the pastry. Roll out the remaining pastry and cut it into a rectangle the same size as the tin; place it over the filling. Brush the top with milk and sprinkle with vanilla sugar. Bake in a preheated oven for 20-25 minutes until lightly golden. When cool, cut into rectangles.

■ COOK'S TIP

Try to avoid using blended vegetable oils as these can contain some saturated fats. Choose instead an unsaturated oil such as corn, sunflower or safflower *which are widely available in major supermarkets.*

■ COOK'S TIP

Vanilla sugar is very easy to make at home. Simply place a whole vanilla pod in a stoppered or screw-topped jar containing caster sugar.

221 SHORTBREAD

Preparation time:
20 minutes

Cooking time:
40 minutes

Oven temperature:
160 C, 325 F, gas 3

**Makes one 20 cm/
8 inch round**

Total Calories:
1,675

YOU WILL NEED:
100 g/4 oz butter
50 g/2 oz caster sugar
175 g/6 oz plain flour, sifted
caster sugar for dusting

Cream the butter and sugar together until light and fluffy. Add the flour and stir until the mixture binds together.

Turn on to a lightly floured board and knead until smooth. Roll out to a 20 cm/8 inch round and place on a greased baking tray. Pinch the edges with your fingers, prick well with a fork and mark into 8 portions.

Dust with caster sugar and bake it in a preheated oven for 40-45 minutes until pale and golden. Leave on the baking tray for 5 minutes, then transfer to a wire rack to cool completely.

222 FLORENTINES

Preparation time:
20 minutes

Cooking time:
8-10 minutes

Oven temperature:
180 C, 350 F, gas 4

Makes 14

Calories:
128 per biscuit

YOU WILL NEED:
75 g/3 oz butter
75 g/3 oz golden syrup
25 g/1 oz plain flour
75 g/3 oz flaked almonds, coarsely
  chopped
25 g/1 oz mixed peel
50 g/2 oz glacé cherries, coarsely
  chopped
1 teaspoon lemon juice
100 g/4 oz plain chocolate

Melt the butter and syrup in a small pan, then stir in the flour, almonds, mixed peel, cherries and lemon juice.

Place teaspoonfuls of the mixture well apart on baking trays lined with baking parchment. Flatten with a fork and bake in a preheated oven for 8-10 minutes. Transfer to a wire rack to cool.

Melt the chocolate in a bowl over a pan of hot water, then spread over the flat underside of each florentine. Place the biscuits chocolate-side up on a wire rack and mark the chocolate into wavy lines with a fork. Leave until set.

◼ COOK'S TIP

The shortbread mixture can be pressed into a special wooden mould before turning out on to the baking tray. These moulds often have a decorative emblem.

◼ COOK'S TIP

Take care not to allow the chocolate to become too hot as this will make it lose its glossy finish. Use the best quality cooking chocolate if possible.

223 ALMOND CURLS

Preparation time:
20 minutes

Cooking time:
6-8 minutes

Oven temperature:
200 C, 400 F, gas 6

Makes 25

Calories:
55 per biscuit

YOU WILL NEED:
75 g/3 oz butter
75 g/3 oz caster sugar
50 g/2 oz plain flour, sifted
75 g/3 oz flaked almonds

Cream the butter and sugar together until light and fluffy. Stir in the flour and almonds and mix well. Place teaspoonfuls of the mixture well apart on greased baking trays and flatten with a damp fork.

Bake in a preheated oven for 6-8 minutes until pale golden. Leave on the baking trays for 1 minute, then remove with a palette knife and place on a rolling pin to curl. Leave until set in a curl, then remove very carefully.

224 COCONUT COOKIES

Preparation time:
20 minutes

Cooking time:
10-15 minutes

Oven temperature:
190 C, 375 F, gas 5

Makes about 40

Calories:
67 per cookie

YOU WILL NEED:
100 g/4 oz butter
175 g/6 oz caster sugar
1 egg, beaten
75 g/3 oz desiccated coconut
175 g/6 oz self-raising flour, sifted

Cream the butter until soft, then add the sugar and beat until light and fluffy. Add the egg and beat thoroughly. Add half the coconut and the flour and stir until mixed. Form into small balls and roll in the remaining coconut.

Place the balls slightly apart on a greased baking tray and flatten each one with a palette knife. Bake in a preheated oven for 10-15 minutes. Transfer to a wire rack to cool.

■ COOK'S TIP

It is a good idea to bake the mixture in a succession of small batches so that the 'curls' do not set before being placed on the rolling pin.

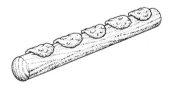

■ COOK'S TIP

Spread the desiccated coconut on a small shallow baking tin and roll each ball of cookie mixture until it is evenly coated before placing on the baking tray.

225 COFFEE KISSES

Preparation time:
30 minutes, plus
cooling

Cooking time:
10 minutes

Oven temperature:
190 C, 375 F, gas 5

Makes about 15

Calories:
164 per biscuit

YOU WILL NEED:
100 g/4 oz butter or margarine
50 g/2 oz caster sugar
150 g/5 oz self-raising flour
3 tablespoons strong black coffee
FOR THE ICING
50 g/2 oz butter, softened
100 g/4 oz icing sugar, sifted
1 tablespoon strong black coffee
icing sugar, for dusting

Beat the butter or margarine and sugar with a wooden spoon for 10 minutes, or in a mixer for 5 minutes, until light and fluffy. Add the flour and coffee and mix to a stiff dough.

Place the mixture in a piping bag, fitted with a large star nozzle. Pipe an even number (about 30) of small stars with the mixture, a little apart, on a greased baking tray.

Bake in a preheated oven for 10 minutes, until just beginning to colour. Cool on the baking tray for 5 minutes, then transfer to a wire rack to cool completely.

To make the icing, beat together the butter, icing sugar and coffee until light and creamy. Sandwich 2 stars together with a little icing, then dust with icing sugar.

226 MACAROONS

Preparation time:
15 minutes, plus
standing

Cooking time:
20 minutes

Oven temperature:
180 C, 350 F, gas 4

Makes 25

Calories:
60 per macaroon

YOU WILL NEED:
225 g/8 oz caster sugar
150 g/5 oz ground almonds
1 tablespoon rice flour
2 egg whites
rice paper
25 split almonds

Mix the sugar, almonds and rice flour together and set aside. Beat the egg whites lightly, add the dry ingredients, and beat to a smooth, firm consistency.

Leave to stand for 5 minutes, then roll into small balls and place slightly apart on a baking tray lined with rice paper. Flatten slightly and place a split almond on each one.

Bake in a preheated oven for 20 minutes. Cool on the baking tray.

■ COOK'S TIP

Flavour the icing with 1 teaspoon of strong black coffee and 2 teaspoons of either brandy or Tia Maria or Crème de Cacao for special occasions.

■ COOK'S TIP

Rice paper is traditionally used to line baking trays for macaroons. Baking parchment is a satisfactory substitute but it is not edible of course.

227 TEA-TIME TRUFFLES

Preparation time:
15 minutes

Makes 15

Calories:
122 per truffle

YOU WILL NEED:
275 g/10 oz cake crumbs
50 g/2 oz caster sugar
2 tablespoons cocoa powder
3 tablespoons apricot jam
1 tablespoon rum
4 tablespoons chocolate vermicelli

Mix the cake crumbs, sugar and cocoa powder together in a bowl. Add the jam and rum and mix to a stiff paste.

Form the mixture into balls the size of a walnut and roll in the chocolate vermicelli. Serve in small paper cases.

228 JAPONAIS

Preparation time:
35-40 minutes

Cooking time:
30-35 minutes

Oven temperature:
150 C, 300 F, gas 2

Makes 8

Calories:
3200 per cake

YOU WILL NEED:
50 g/2 oz ground almonds
100 g/4 oz caster sugar
2 egg whites
25 g/1 oz ground almonds, browned
8 hazelnuts, toasted and skinned
FOR THE BUTTER ICING
75 g/3 oz butter
175 g/6 oz icing sugar, sifted
1 teaspoon coffee essence
1 tablespoon milk
FOR THE GLACE ICING
100 g/4 oz icing sugar, sifted
1 teaspoon coffee essence
2 teaspoons water

Mix the almonds and sugar together and set aside. Whisk the egg whites until stiff, then fold in the almonds and sugar. Spoon the mixture into a piping bag fitted with a 1 cm/½ inch plain nozzle and pipe sixteen 5 cm/2 inch rounds on a baking tray lined with baking parchment. Bake in a preheated oven for 30-35 minutes. Transfer to a wire rack to cool.

To make the butter icing, cream the butter with half the icing sugar until soft, then add the milk, essence and remaining icing sugar. Sandwich the rounds together in pairs with some of the icing and spread more round the sides.

To make the glacé icing, mix the icing sugar with the coffee essence and water. Press ground almonds round the side of each cake (see Cook's Tip). Place a little glacé icing on top. When set, decorate with piped butter icing and nuts.

■ COOK'S TIP

Crumbs from a Madeira sponge cake are the ideal choice for making these truffles but crumbs from a plain chocolate sponge may also be used.

■ COOK'S TIP

Spread the ground almonds out on a plate. Hold each cake centrally between forefinger and thumb and roll carefully through the ground almonds to coat.

229 COCONUT LOAF

Preparation time:
15 minutes

Cooking time:
1-1¼ hours

Oven temperature:
180 C, 350 F, gas 4

**Makes one 450 g/
1 lb loaf**

Total calories:
2,182

YOU WILL NEED:
100 g/4 oz butter or margarine
100 g/4 oz caster sugar
2 eggs
175 g/6 oz self-raising flour, sifted
4 tablespoons desiccated coconut
2 tablespoons milk

Cream the fat and sugar together until light and fluffy. Beat in the eggs one at a time, adding a little of the flour with the second. Fold in the remaining flour, 3 tablespoons of the coconut and the milk.

Turn into a lined and greased 450 g/1 lb loaf tin and sprinkle with the remaining coconut. Bake in a preheated oven for 1-1¼ hours. Turn out and cool on a wire rack.

230 PARKIN

Preparation time:
15 minutes

Cooking time:
50-60 minutes

Oven temperature:
180 C, 350 F, gas 4

**Makes one 20 cm/
8 inch square cake**

Total calories:
3,687

YOU WILL NEED:
225 g/8 oz wholemeal flour
225 g/8 oz rolled oats
½ teaspoon bicarbonate of soda
½ teaspoon salt
1 teaspoon ground ginger
100 g/4 oz butter
100 g/4 oz black treacle
100 g/4 oz golden syrup
100 g/4 oz soft brown sugar
175 ml/6 fl oz milk

Place the flour and oats in a mixing bowl and sift in the soda, salt and ginger. Place the butter, treacle, syrup and sugar in a saucepan and heat gently. Cool slightly, then add to the dry ingredients, together with the milk; mix thoroughly.

Pour into a lined and greased 20 cm/8 inch square cake tin and bake in a preheated oven for 50-60 minutes until the cake is firm to the touch.

Leave in the tin for 15 minutes, then turn on to a wire rack to cool. Store in an airtight tin for several days before eating.

■ COOK'S TIP

When a cake is nearly cooked, the mixture tends to shrink slightly from the tin. If a fine skewer inserted in the centre comes out clean, the cake is ready.

■ COOK'S TIP

By baking the parkin in a square cake tin, it is much easier to divide into equal portions – an advantage if making this for a fund-raising coffee morning.

231 BANANA CAKE

Preparation time:
30 minutes

Cooking time:
20-25 minutes

Oven temperature:
180 C, 350 F, gas 4

**Makes one 18 cm/
7 inch cake**

Total calories:
2,480

YOU WILL NEED:
100 g/4 oz butter or margarine
100 g/4 oz caster sugar
2 eggs
100 g/4 oz self-raising flour, sifted
2 bananas, mashed
icing sugar, to dust
FOR THE FILLING
50 g/2 oz ground almonds
50 g/2 oz icing sugar, sifted
1 small banana, mashed
½ teaspoon lemon juice

Cream the fat and sugar together until light and fluffy. Add the eggs one at a time, adding a tablespoon of flour with the second egg. Fold in the remaining flour with the bananas.

Divide the mixture between two 18 cm/7 inch greased and lined sandwich tins. Bake in a preheated oven for 20-25 minutes until the cakes spring back when lightly pressed. Turn on to a wire rack to cool.

To make the filling, mix the ground almonds with the icing sugar, then add the banana and lemon juice and mix to a smooth paste. Sandwich the cakes together with the filling and dust thickly with icing sugar.

232 CHOCOLATE BISCUIT CAKE

Preparation time:
20 minutes, plus
chilling

**Makes one 20 cm/
8 inch round**

Total calories:
3,612

YOU WILL NEED:
100 g/4 oz margarine
50 g/2 oz caster sugar
2 tablespoons golden syrup
2 tablespoons milk
2 tablespoons drinking chocolate
1 tablespoon cocoa powder
225 g/8 oz digestive biscuits, crushed
50 g/2 oz cake crumbs
50 g/2 oz glacé cherries, chopped
50 g/2 oz raisins
FOR THE ICING
100 g/4 oz plain chocolate
15 g/½ oz butter

Place the margarine, sugar, syrup and milk in a pan and heat gently. Add the drinking chocolate, cocoa and half the biscuits and mix well. Add the remaining ingredients and stir until thoroughly mixed, then press into a 20 cm/8 inch sandwich tin. Chill in the refrigerator until set, then remove from the tin.

Melt the chocolate and butter in a small bowl over a pan of hot water and mix well. Spread over the biscuit mixture and allow to set, then cut into wedges.

■ COOK'S TIP

A quick way to decorate a cake with a level top is to sift icing sugar through a lacy doily laid over it. Remove the doily carefully to reveal the pattern.

■ COOK'S TIP

A 20 cm/8 inch flan ring set over a baking tray can be used instead of a sandwich tin. Check first that the baking tray fits into the refrigerator.

233 MADEIRA CAKE

Preparation time:
20 minutes

Cooking time:
1½ hours

Oven temperature:
160 C, 325 F, gas 3

**Makes one 15 cm/
6 inch cake**

Total calories:
2,964

YOU WILL NEED:
175 g/6 oz butter
175 g/6 oz caster sugar
3 eggs, beaten
225 g/8 oz plain flour
1 teaspoon baking powder
grated rind of ½ lemon
strip of citron peel (optional)

Grease and line the base of a 15 cm/6 inch round cake tin.

Beat the butter and sugar with a wooden spoon for 10 minutes, or in a mixer for 5 minutes, until light and fluffy. Beat in the eggs, a little at a time. Sift the flour and baking powder into the bowl. Fold them into the mixture using a metal spoon. Fold in the lemon rind.

Place the mixture in the prepared tin. Smooth the top. If using, place the strip of citron peel in the centre of the cake. Bake in a preheated oven for 1½ hours until the cake has risen and is light golden in colour. When cooked the cake should spring back when pressed with the fingers. Turn out and cool on a wire rack.

■ COOK'S TIP

Wrapped tightly in foil, this cake will keep fresh for a week. It can be dusted with sifted icing sugar before serving instead of decorating with peel.

234 CRYSTALLIZED FRUIT CAKE

Preparation time:
30 minutes

Cooking time:
3 hours

Oven temperature:
160 C, 325 F, gas 3,
then
150 C, 300 F, gas 2

**Makes one 18 cm/
7 inch cake**

Total calories:
4,806

YOU WILL NEED:
175 g/6 oz butter
175 g/6 oz soft brown sugar
225 g/8 oz plain flour
1 teaspoon ground mixed spice
3 eggs
225 g/8 oz raisins
100 g/4 oz sultanas
25 g/1 oz angelica
100 g/4 oz glacé cherries, quartered
25 g/1 oz crystallized ginger
1 tablespoon sherry
75 g/3 oz crystallized fruits
50 g/2 oz walnuts
2 tablespoons apricot jam
1 tablespoon water
squeeze of lemon juice

Grease and line the base and side of a deep 18 cm/7 inch cake tin with baking parchment. Cream the butter and sugar together until light and fluffy. Sift the flour with the mixed spice. Beat the eggs one at a time into the creamed butter and sugar, adding a tablespoon of the flour with the last two. Fold in the remaining flour with the fruit, ginger and sherry. Turn into the prepared tin and decorate with the crystallized fruits and walnuts. Bake in a preheated moderate oven for 1 hour, then lower the temperature and bake for a further 2 hours. Leave in the tin for 5 minutes, then turn out to cool.

Simmer the jam and water for 3-4 minutes. Stir in the lemon juice, then sieve. Brush over the fruit.

■ COOK'S TIP

For special occasions, arrange the crystallized fruits and walnuts artistically on the top of the cake – in the shape of a flower, for example.

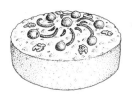

235 STICKY GINGERBREAD

Preparation time:
15 minutes

Cooking time:
50 minutes

Oven temperature:
180 C, 350 F, gas 4

Makes about 15 pieces

Calories:
227 per portion

YOU WILL NEED:
275 g/10 oz plain flour
2 teaspoons ground ginger
1 teaspoon bicarbonate of soda
100 g/4 oz margarine
100 g/4 oz soft light brown sugar
225 g/8 oz golden syrup
100 g/4 oz black treacle
2 eggs, beaten
150 ml/¼ pint hot water

Grease and line a 30 × 23 cm/12 × 9 inch roasting tin with baking parchment.

Sift the flour, ginger and bicarbonate of soda into a large mixing bowl. Heat the margarine, sugar, syrup and treacle gently in a saucepan until the margarine has melted and the sugar has dissolved.

Make a well in the centre of the dry ingredients. Pour the margarine into the flour and beat well to mix. Add the beaten eggs and hot water and mix to a smooth batter. Pour the mixture into the prepared tin.

Bake in a preheated oven for 45 minutes or until the cake springs back when pressed with the fingers. Turn out of the tin, remove the paper and cool on a wire rack.

■ COOK'S TIP

Keep this gingerbread for 2 days before eating. Cut into slices to serve. If required, it can be stored for up to 2 weeks wrapped in greaseproof paper, then foil.

236 ANGEL CAKE

Preparation time:
20 minutes

Cooking time:
35-40 minutes

Oven temperature:
180 C, 350 F, gas 4

Makes one 20 cm/ 8 inch cake

Total calories: 851

YOU WILL NEED:
25 g/1 oz plain flour
25 g/1 oz cornflour
150 g/5 oz caster sugar
5 large egg whites
1 teaspoon vanilla essence
icing sugar, for dusting

Sift the flours and 25 g/1 oz of the caster sugar together 3 or 4 times. Whisk the egg whites until stiff, add the remaining caster sugar a tablespoon at a time and continue whisking until very thick.

Carefully fold in the sifted mixture with the vanilla essence and turn into a 20 cm/8 inch angel cake tin. Smooth the surface and bake in a preheated oven for 35-40 minutes, until the cake springs back when lightly pressed.

Turn it upside down on a wire rack and leave in the tin until cold when the tin can easily be removed. Serve dusted thickly with icing sugar.

■ COOK'S TIP

Some specialist kitchen equipment shops offer a hire service for unusual shapes and sizes of cake tins such as the fluted one with sloping sides used here.

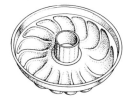

237 COFFEE AND WALNUT LAYER CAKE

Preparation time: 30 minutes	YOU WILL NEED:
	4 eggs
Cooking time: 30-35 minutes	*175 g/6 oz caster sugar*
	100 g/4 oz plain flour, sifted
	1 tablespoon oil
Oven temperature: 190 C, 375 F, gas 5	*100 g/4 oz walnuts, finely chopped*
	walnut halves, to decorate
	FOR THE BUTTER ICING
Makes one 20cm/ 8 inch cake	*225 g/8 oz butter*
	450 g/1 lb icing sugar, sifted
Total calories: 5,416	*2 tablespoons milk*
	2 tablespoons coffee essence

Line and grease two 20 cm/8 inch sandwich tins. Whisk the eggs and sugar in a bowl over a pan of boiling water until thick enough to leave a trail. (If using an electric beater, the hot water is unnecessary.) Partially fold in the flour, then add the oil and chopped walnuts and fold in gently. Divide the mixture between the prepared tins and bake in a preheated oven for 30-35 minutes until the cakes spring back when lightly pressed. Turn on to a wire rack to cool. Split each cake in half.

To make the butter icing, cream the butter with half the icing sugar until soft, then add the milk, essence and remaining icing sugar. Beat well.

Spread a quarter of the icing on to three of the cake rounds and sandwich the cake together. Swirl the remaining icing over the cake and decorate with walnut halves.

238 STRAWBERRY CREAM SPONGE

Preparation time: 20 minutes	YOU WILL NEED:
	3 eggs
Cooking time: 20-25 minutes	*75 g/3 oz caster sugar*
	75 g/3 oz plain flour
	25 g/1 oz butter, melted
Oven temperature: 180 C, 350 F, gas 4	*icing sugar, to dust*
	FOR THE FILLING
Makes one 20 cm/ 8 inch cake	*150 ml/¼ pint double cream*
	225 g/8 oz strawberries, sliced

Total calories: 1,791

Grease and line two 20 cm/8 inch sandwich tins with baking parchment or greaseproof paper.

Place the eggs and caster sugar in a bowl over hot water and whisk with an electric whisk for about 10 minutes until the mixture is light and thick and leaves a trail when the whisk is lifted. Sift the flour into a bowl and fold in lightly, using a metal spoon, until evenly mixed. Pour the melted butter slowly into the mixture and fold in. Pour the mixture into the prepared tins and level the surface.

Bake in a preheated oven for 20-25 minutes until the cakes are golden brown and firm to the touch. Turn out on to a wire rack and leave to cool.

To serve, whip the cream, place one cake on a serving plate and spread with the cream. Cover with the strawberries. Place the second cake on top and sift over the icing sugar.

■ COOK'S TIP

Walnuts can become rancid quite quickly, so always buy in small quantities from shops with a rapid turnover. Use a palette knife to swirl the icing over the cake.

■ COOK'S TIP

Fresh raspberries can be used instead of strawberries to give a slightly sharper taste to the filling. The sponge layers can be made in advance, packed in
polythene bags and frozen for up to 3 months. To thaw, leave in the bags at room temperature for about 1 hour.

239 NUTTY BROWN SUGAR MERINGUES

Preparation time:
30 minutes, plus
cooling

Cooking time:
6-8 hours or
overnight

Oven temperature:
110 C, 225 F, gas ¼

Makes 10

Calories:
68 per meringue

YOU WILL NEED:
2 egg whites
100 g/4 oz soft light brown sugar
25 g/1 oz chopped mixed nuts
150 ml/¼ pint whipping cream
1 teaspoon icing sugar
few drops of vanilla essence

Line a baking tray with baking parchment or lightly greased greasproof paper.

Whisk the egg whites in a bowl until stiff. Sprinkle over 50 g/2 oz of the sugar and whisk again until very stiff and glossy. Lightly fold in the remaining sugar, using a large metal spoon. Put the mixture into a piping bag fitted with a large star nozzle, and pipe 20 star shapes on to the prepared baking tray. Sprinkle with nuts. Bake the meringues in a preheated oven for 6-8 hours, or overnight, until completely dried out. Transfer to a wire rack to cool.

Whip the cream with the icing sugar and vanilla essence to taste until stiff peaks form. Use to sandwich the meringues together in pairs. Serve within 30 minutes of assembling.

■ COOK'S TIP

If making these meringues in advance, leave to cool for 15 minutes only, then store in polythene bags in an airtight tin for up to 6 weeks.

240 BLACK FOREST GATEAU

Preparation time:
1 hour, plus
overnight soaking

Cooking time:
30-40 minutes

Oven temperature:
190 C, 375 F, gas 5

**Makes one 20 cm/
8 inch cake**

Total calories:
5,357

YOU WILL NEED:
6 eggs
175 g/6 oz caster sugar
*175 g/6 oz plain flour, sifted with
50 g/2 oz cocoa powder*
8 tablespoons cherry brandy
*2 × 450 g/1 lb cans black cherries,
drained, stoned and halved, juice
reserved*
600 ml/1 pint double cream, whipped
*2 teaspoons arrowroot, slaked with
water*
75 g/3 oz plain chocolate, grated

Grease and flour two 20 cm/8 inch round cake tins. Place the eggs and the sugar in a bowl over a pan of simmering water and whisk until they form a trail. Remove the bowl from the pan and whisk until the mixture is cool. Fold in the flour mixture gently. Divide between the tins and bake in a preheated oven for 30-40 minutes.

Leave the cakes to cool in the tins. Turn out on to wire racks. Split the cakes in half horizontally when cold. Sprinkle 4 tablespoons of both the cherry brandy and cherry juice on each layer. Soak overnight. Sandwich a third of the cream and half the black cherries between each layer. Spread half the remaining cream around the sides. Arrange the remaining cherries on the top, leaving a border for rosettes of whipped cream. Slake the arrowroot into the reserved cherry juice. Bring gently to the boil, stirring until the sauce clears and thickens, then pour over cherries. Pipe cream rosettes round the edge and cover the sides with the chocolate.

■ COOK'S TIP

Chocolate scrolls make an attractive alternative to grated chocolate. Softened chocolate can be piped in varied scroll shapes on waxed paper – they are *easily lifted off with a knife when set. Some cake decorating shops sell chocolate scrolls.*

COCKTAIL PARTIES

For a party of thirty guests, offer a choice of six or eight different items. Ideally, serve a platter of hot canapés about half-way through the party. Do not attempt to make more than one variety unless there is some-one to help in the kitchen. Don't forget to have plenty of ice in reserve for the drinks.

241 ANGELS ON HORSEBACK

Preparation time:	YOU WILL NEED:
20 minutes	12 oysters, shelled
	3 tablespoons lemon juice
Cooking time:	salt
5-10 minutes	cayenne
Makes 12	12 rashers rindless streaky bacon
	juice of 1 lemon
Calories:	1 large bunch of watercress, to garnish
12 per angel	

Dip the oysters in the lemon juice and sprinkle with salt and cayenne. Stretch the bacon with the blade of a knife, then wrap each oyster in a rasher. Secure with wooden cocktail sticks.

Cook under a preheated hot grill for 5-10 minutes or until the bacon is golden and crisp. Arrange on a serving platter garnished with watercress, sprinkle with lemon juice and serve immediately. If liked, put the 'angels' on triangles of fried bread.

242 LAMB AND MINT MEATBALLS

Preparation time:	YOU WILL NEED:
20 minutes	450 g/1 lb lean minced lamb
	2 garlic cloves, crushed
Cooking time:	2 teaspoons mint sauce
about 30 minutes	salt and pepper
Makes about 25	1 egg, beaten
	oil for shallow frying
Calories:	parsley sprigs, to garnish
62 per meatball	FOR THE DIP
	50 g/2 oz demerara sugar
	2 teaspoons cornflour
	3 tablespoons water
	4 tablespoons redcurrant jelly
	2 tablespoons Worcestershire sauce

Put the lamb in a bowl and add the garlic and mint sauce. Season well with salt and pepper and bind the mixture with the eggs. With floured hands, roll into walnut-sized balls.

Heat the oil in a frying pan, add the meatballs in batches and fry for about 10 minutes until golden brown. Drain on absorbent kitchen paper and keep warm.

To make the dip, put the sugar, cornflour and water in a small pan and blend in the redcurrant jelly and Worcestershire sauce. Bring slowly to the boil and cook stirring, until smooth.

Spear the meatballs on to cocktail sticks. Garnish with parsley and serve warm, with the dip.

■ COOK'S TIP

Angels on horseback are classic cocktail appetizers but as oysters are now so expensive, only serve them at a small party to celebrate a special occasion! Try combining a selection of 'angels' and 'devils' (see recipe 250) on a serving platter.

■ COOK'S TIP

The dip can be made in advance and reheated in a bowl over a saucepan of simmering water just before serving. The meatballs can also be prepared in advance.

243 POTATO SKINS WITH SOURED CREAM

Preparation time:
15 minutes, plus chilling

Cooking time:
1½-1¾ hours

Oven temperature:
190 C, 375 F, gas 5

Makes 20

Total calories: 920

YOU WILL NEED:
5 large potatoes, scrubbed and dried
150 ml/¼ pint soured cream
1 teaspoon snipped fresh chives
salt and pepper
vegetable oil

Prick the potatoes with a fork and bake for about 1¼ hours until tender. Meanwhile prepare the dip. Mix the soured cream with the chives and salt and pepper to taste. Spoon into a bowl, cover and chill.

Leave the potatoes to cool for a few minutes, then cut each one lengthways into 4 long pieces. Using a teaspoon scoop out most of the potato, leaving just a thin layer next to the skin. (Use the potato as a topping for a vegetable pie.)

Pour vegetable oil into a small pan to a depth of 7.5 cm/3 inches. Heat the oil to 180-190 C/350-375 F. Fry 4-5 potato skins at a time for about 2 minutes until brown and crisp. Lift from the oil with a slotted spoon and drain on absorbent kitchen paper. Keep the skins hot in the oven while the remaining skins are cooked. Sprinkle the skins lightly with salt and serve with the chilled soured cream dip.

244 TUNA AND PARMESAN PUFFS

Preparation time:
45 minutes

Cooking time:
15-18 minutes

Oven temperature:
200 C, 400 F, gas 6

Makes about 150

Total calories:
1,925

YOU WILL NEED:
150 ml/¼ pint water
50 g/2 oz butter
75 g/3 oz plain flour, sifted
2 eggs, beaten
25 g/1 oz grated Parmesan cheese
parsley sprigs, to garnish
FOR THE FILLING
1 × 200g can tuna fish, drained
6 tablespoons mayonnaise

Heat the water and butter slowly in a pan until the butter has melted. Remove from the heat, quickly add all the flour and beat until the mixture leaves the side of the pan. Add the eggs gradually, beating thoroughly between each addition. Beat in the cheese.

Spoon the mixture into a piping bag fitted with a 1 cm/½ inch nozzle and pipe tiny mounds on to a large moistened baking tray, spacing them well apart. Bake in a preheated oven for 12-15 minutes, until crisp and golden.

Meanwhile, mash the tuna fish with the mayonnaise. Make a small slit in the side of each puff and spoon a little of the tuna mixture into each. Serve warm, garnished with parsley.

COOK'S TIP

If you do not have a thermometer, test the temperature of the oil with a cube of bread. If the temperature is high enough, the bread should brown in 30 seconds. Strain the oil before pouring back into its container for future use.

COOK'S TIP

A good way of improving your piping skills is to practise with instant mashed potato mixed to the required consistency.

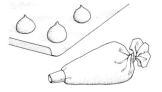

245 PARMA HAM NIBBLES

Preparation time:
25 minutes

Makes 59

Calories:
13 per portion

YOU WILL NEED:
about 15 thin slices of Parma ham,
*   total weight about 225 g/8 oz*
3 kiwi fruit
⅓ Ogen or honeydew melon
½ fresh pineapple
½ white cabbage, to serve (optional)

Cut each slice of Parma ham into long strips about 2.5 cm/
1 inch wide. You should get 4 strips from each slice.

Peel the kiwi fruit and cut each one in half lengthways,
then cut each half into 3 long wedges, giving 18 pieces alto-
gether. Remove the seeds from the melon and cut it into 10
thin slices about 1-2 cm/½-¾ inch thick. Remove the skin and
cut each slice in half. Cut the pineapple into 7 slices and remove the skin. Cut each slice into 3 wedges giving 21 pieces in
all.

Wrap a piece of Parma ham around each piece of fruit
and spear it with a cocktail stick. Arrange the nibbles in rows
on a fairly large plate or tray or stick them into half a cabbage
positioned on a plate. Cover with cling film until required.

246 JAPANESE ALMONDS

Preparation time:
5 minutes

Cooking time:
35-40 minutes

Oven temperature:
150 C, 300 F, gas 2

Serves 16

Calories:
230 per portion

YOU WILL NEED:
625 g/1¼ lb blanched almonds
50 g/2 oz butter
2 tablespoons soy sauce
2 tablespoons dry sherry
½ teaspoon ground ginger
garlic salt

Spread the almonds in a shallow baking tin and toast in a preheated oven for 20 minutes.

Meanwhile, melt the butter in a saucepan. Stir in the soy
sauce, sherry and ginger. Pour over the almonds and continue
toasting, stirring occasionally, for 15-20 minutes. Sprinkle
with garlic salt to taste, then spread out on absorbent kitchen
paper and leave to dry and cool.

■ COOK'S TIP

Remove any discoloured or
blemished outer leaves from
the cabbage. Make sure that
you cut it straight through
the centre so that the half
has a perfectly flat base.

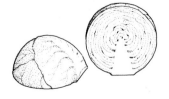

■ COOK'S TIP

Place the almonds in small
bowls and position in
different parts of the room
so that your guests can help
themselves. Keep some in
reserve for late arrivals.

247 SMOKED SALMON AND CRESS PINWHEELS

Preparation time: about 25 minutes, plus chilling

Makes 48

Calories: 38 per portion

YOU WILL NEED:
150 ml/¼ pint thick mayonnaise
salt and pepper
grated rind of ¼ lemon
1 teaspoon lemon juice
2 cartons mustard and cress, chopped
8 thinly cut slices of very fresh brown bread
100 g/4 oz thinly sliced smoked salmon
FOR THE GARNISH
sprigs of parsley
lemon quarters

Combine the mayonnaise, salt, pepper, lemon rind, lemon juice and chopped mustard and cress.

Cut the crusts off the bread and spread each slice evenly with cress mayonnaise. Cut pieces of the smoked salmon to fit each slice of bread leaving 1 cm/½ inch uncovered at one end of each slice. Carefully roll up the slices of bread, beginning at the plain end. Wrap each roll tightly in cling film and chill for at least 1 hour and up to 12 hours before serving.

To serve, unwrap the rolls and cut each one into 6 slices. Arrange them on a plate and garnish with parsley and lemon.

248 SATAY WITH PEANUT SAUCE

Preparation time: 30 minutes

Cooking time: about 2 minutes

Makes about 20

Calories: 30 per portion

YOU WILL NEED:
350 g/12 oz pork fillet
1 teaspoon chilli powder
5 tablespoons water
1 tablespoon oil
1 onion, grated
1 garlic clove, crushed
2 tablespoons lemon juice
5 tablespoons water
4 tablespoons crunchy peanut butter
1 teaspoon salt
1 teaspoon ground cumin
1 teaspoon ground coriander

Cut the pork fillet into small dice and thread 3 or 4 pieces on one end of about 20 wooden cocktail sticks. Cook under a preheated hot grill for 1 minute on each side, or until cooked through. Drain on absorbent kitchen paper and keep warm.

Blend the chilli powder and 1 teaspoon of the water together to make a paste. Heat the oil in a pan, add the onion, garlic and chilli paste and fry gently until the onion is soft. Add the remaining ingredients, stirring well to combine. Transfer to a serving bowl.

Serve the satay with the sauce.

■ COOK'S TIP

Very fresh bread can be difficult to cut thinly. It is easier if you dip the knife in boiling water and shake off the drips before cutting each slice. Just steady the loaf with one hand – do not press on it as a really fresh loaf will not spring back into shape.

■ COOK'S TIP

Small dice of skinless chicken breast can be used instead of some of the pork fillet. Brush lightly with oil before cooking under the grill.

249 DEMON DATES

Preparation time:
30 minutes

Cooking time:
8-10 minutes

Makes 40

Calories:
70 per date

YOU WILL NEED:
40 fresh dates, total weight about
 750 g/1½ lb
40 hickory smoked whole almonds or
 toasted whole almonds
40 rindless short rashers streaky
 bacon
parsley sprig, to garnish

Remove the stones from the dates and replace them with the almonds.

Stretch the bacon a little with the back of a knife and then wrap 1 rasher around each date and thread them on to a long metal skewer, placing about 10 dates on each skewer.

When you are ready to serve, put the skewers under a preheated moderate grill and cook them for 4-5 minutes on each side until the bacon is well browned. Remove them from the skewers and serve warm. Garnish with a sprig of parsley.

250 DEVILS ON HORSEBACK

Preparation time:
25 minutes

Cooking time:
10-12 minutes

Makes 20

Calories:
62 per portion

YOU WILL NEED:
25 g/1 oz butter
1 onion, finely chopped
1 teaspoon dried sage
50 g/2 oz fresh breadcrumbs
225 g/8 oz prunes, stoned
10 rashers rindless streaky bacon

Melt the butter in a pan, add the onion and fry gently until soft. Stir in the sage and breadcrumbs. Stuff the prunes with this mixture.

Stretch the bacon with the back of a knife, then cut each rasher in half. Wrap each prune in a piece of bacon and secure with a wooden cocktail stick. Place under a preheated grill and cook for 4-5 minutes on each side, until the bacon is crisp.

■ COOK'S TIP

If fresh dates are not
available, you can use 2
boxes of dessert dates. If
they are very sticky, place
them in a sieve and pour
boiling water over them.

■ COOK'S TIP

Devils on horseback may be
the poor relation of 'angels'
(see recipe 241) but they are
delicious! Preferably use
prunes that do not require
any soaking before use.

251 CHEESE AND ANCHOVY AIGRETTES

Preparation time:
30 minutes

Cooking time:
30 minutes

Makes about 50

Calories:
49 per portion

YOU WILL NEED:
50 g/2 oz butter
150 ml/¼ pint water
65 g/2½ oz plain flour, sifted
pinch of salt
2 eggs, beaten
2 tablespoons grated Parmesan cheese
50 g/2 oz Cheddar cheese, grated
1 × 50 g/2 oz can anchovy fillets,
    drained and chopped
deep oil, for frying
parsley sprig, to garnish
whisky mayonnaise (see Cook's Tip)

Melt the butter in the water in a pan, then bring to the boil. Add the flour and salt all at once and beat until the mixture forms a smooth paste which leaves the sides of the pan clean. Leave to cool slightly. Gradually beat in the egg, incorporating as much air as possible until the mixture is smooth and glossy; then beat in the two cheeses and the anchovies.

Heat the oil in a deep fryer or a deep saucepan to 180 C/350 F or until a cube of bread browns in 30 seconds. Put the aigrette mixture into a piping bag fitted with a plain 2 cm/¾ inch vegetable nozzle. Pipe out lengths about 2-2.5 cm/¾-1 inch long and drop them carefully into the hot oil. Cook about 12 at a time for 4-5 minutes, until golden brown and crisp, turning them over, if necesary. Drain the aigrettes on absorbent kitchen paper and keep them warm while frying the remainder. Garnish with parsley and serve warm or cold.

■ COOK'S TIP

For the whisky mayonnaise, whisk together 1 egg yolk and ½ teaspoon dry mustard. Whisk in 150 ml/¼ pint sunflower oil, drop by drop, until half has been incorporated. Beat in 1 teaspoon lemon juice, then gradually add the remaining oil. Add 1 tablespoon whisky, ½ teaspoon caster sugar, and salt and pepper.

252 CRUDITES WITH CHEESE AND ONION DIP

Preparation time:
25-30 minutes, plus
chilling

Serves 10

Calories:
120 per portion

YOU WILL NEED:
2 large carrots, cut into sticks
⅓ cucumber, cut into sticks
2 courgettes, trimmed and sliced
100 g/4 oz button mushrooms, halved
1 bunch radishes, trimmed
FOR THE DIP
100 g/4 oz full-fat soft cream cheese
2 tablespoons mayonnaise
salt and pepper
75 g/3 oz mature Cheddar cheese,
    finely grated
½ bunch spring onions, trimmed and
    sliced or chopped

To make the dip, beat the cream cheese until soft, then beat in the mayonnaise and season with salt and pepper. Finally beat in the Cheddar cheese and the spring onions, reserving a few for garnish.

Turn into a small bowl, cover with cling film and chill for at least 2 hours.

Place the bowl of dip in the centre of a serving platter and garnish with the reserved spring onions. Arrange the crudités decoratively on the platter.

■ COOK'S TIP

The choice of vegetables depends on availability and personal preferences. Small florets of cauliflower and short lengths of celery are also very suitable.

253 CHEESE STRAWS

Preparation time:
25-30 minutes, plus chilling

Cooking time:
10-15 minutes

Oven temperature:
200 C, 400 F, gas 6

Makes about 40

Total calories: 1,110

YOU WILL NEED:
100 g/4 oz plain flour
salt
pinch of cayenne
50 g/2 oz butter
50 g/2 oz Cheddar cheese, finely grated
1 egg yolk, beaten

Sift the flour and seasonings together in a mixing bowl. Add the butter in pieces and rub together with the fingertips until the mixture resembes fine breadcrumbs. Stir in the grated cheese and the egg yolk. Draw together with the fingertips to form a smooth dough, using a little cold water if the mixture is too dry. Chill for at least 30 minutes.

Roll out the dough thinly on a floured board and cut into strips about 12.5 cm/5 inches long and 5 mm/¼ inch wide. Place on baking trays and bake in a preheated oven for 10-15 minutes or until golden. Remove from the oven, allow to cool slightly, then transfer to a wire rack to cool completely. Store in an airtight tin.

254 CHIVE BISCUITS WITH SAGE CREAM

Preparation time:
30-35 minutes, plus chilling

Cooking time:
10 minutes

Oven temperature:
220 C, 425 F, gas 7

Makes about 100

Total calories:
1,798

YOU WILL NEED:
100 g/4 oz butter
125 g/4½ oz creamy soft cheese
100 g/4 oz plain flour, sifted
1 tablespoon chopped chives
FOR THE SAGE CREAM
100 g/4 oz Sage Derby cheese
100 g/4 oz curd cheese
4 tablespoons natural yogurt
salt and pepper
green food colouring (optional)

Cream the butter and cheese together until well blended. Stir in the flour and chives and mix with a fork until well combined. Roll the dough into a ball and wrap in cling film. Chill for at least 1 hour.

Roll out to a 5 mm/¼ inch thickness and cut into 4 cm/1½ inch rounds with a plain cutter. Place well apart on greased baking trays and bake in a preheated oven for 10 minutes. Cool on a wire rack.

To make the sage cream, beat the ingredients together until smooth, with salt and pepper to taste and a few drops of colouring if liked. Put the mixture into a piping bag fitted with a 1 cm/½ inch star nozzle. Pipe on the biscuits.

▪ COOK'S TIP

Use a mature Cheddar if you like a more pronounced taste of cheese and sprinkle a little paprika over them before serving. These straws are also good to hand round with drinks before a meal as they are not too filling.

▪ COOK'S TIP

If you feel uneasy about using a piping bag, spread the sage cream quite thickly over half the biscuits and cover with the remaining biscuits.

255 SEEDED BISCUITS

Preparation time:
10 minutes

Cooking time:
about 5 minutes

Oven temperature:
180 C, 350 F, gas 4

Makes 24

Calories:
51 per biscuit

YOU WILL NEED:
24 small water biscuits
50 g/2 oz butter, melted
caraway, poppy or sesame seeds

Brush one side of each biscuit with melted butter. Sprinkle with caraway, poppy or sesame seeds and arrange the biscuits on baking trays. Heat in a preheated oven for 5 minutes or until crisp and hot.

256 SPICED ALMONDS

Preparation time:
5 minutes

Cooking time:
about 5 minutes

Makes 100 g/4 oz

Total calories: 575

YOU WILL NEED:
3 tablespoons sunflower oil
100 g/4 oz flaked almonds
1 teaspoon salt
1 teaspoon curry powder

Heat the oil in a frying pan, add the almonds and fry until golden brown. Drain on abosrbent kitchen paper, then place in a serving dish.

Mix the salt and curry powder together and sprinkle over the almonds; toss well to coat.

■ COOK'S TIP

Most health food shops sell a variety of different seeds in small quantities. Not everyone likes the distinctive flavour of caraway so it could be a good idea to try sprinkling some of the biscuits with poppy or sesame seeds too.

■ COOK'S TIP

Keen cooks should have a collection of different types of oil. Sunflower oil is excellent for frying the almonds in this recipe.

257 AVOCADO DIP

Preparation time:
15-20 minutes, plus chilling

Serves 8

Calories:
154 per portion

YOU WILL NEED:
2 ripe avocados
juice of 1 lemon
2 tablespoons olive oil
1 small onion, finely chopped
1 garlic clove, crushed with ½
    teaspoon salt
225 g/8 oz tomatoes, skinned, seeded
    and finely chopped
dash of Tabasco sauce
freshly chopped parsley, to garnish

Cut the avocados in half with a sharp, stainless steel knife. Remove the stones and scoop out the flesh into a bowl. Mash the lemon juice into the flesh with a fork. Add the remaining ingredients and blend well together until the dip is quite smooth. Cover with cling film and chill for at least 2 hours.

Transfer to a serving dish and top with plenty of freshly chopped parsley before serving.

258 CURRIED EGG DIP

Preparation time:
10 minutes, plus chilling

Serves 8

Calories:
58 per portion

YOU WILL NEED:
2 tablespoons soured cream
2 tablespoons mayonnaise
1 teaspoon curry powder
2 hard-boiled eggs, finely chopped
1 tablespoon chopped fresh parsley,
    plus some for garnish
1-2 teaspoons lemon juice
curry powder, to garnish

Beat together the soured cream, mayonnaise and curry powder; then beat in the eggs and parsley, season with salt and pepper to taste and add sufficient lemon juice to give a dipping consistency.

Turn the dip into a small bowl and cover with cling film. Chill for at least 2 hours.

For serving, place the bowl in the centre of a large plate, sprinkle the dip with curry powder and chopped parsley and surround with tortilla crisps.

■ COOK'S TIP

If the dip is to be made in advance, store it in the refrigerator with the avocado stones buried in the mixture, and keep the dish tightly covered.

■ COOK'S TIP

Most supermarkets sell packets of tortilla crisps. They are ideal for serving with spicy dips. Their triangular shape makes them easy to use.

259 DEVILLED DIP

Preparation time:
20 minutes, plus
chilling

Serves 10

Calories:
170 per portion

YOU WILL NEED:
225 g/8 oz cottage cheese
150 ml/¼ pint thick mayonnaise
100 g/4 oz mixed nuts and raisins,
    finely chopped
1 green pepper, cored, seeded and
    finely chopped
1 teaspoon Tabasco sauce
pinch of cayenne
salt and pepper

Mix the cottage cheese and mayonnaise together in a bowl. Stir in the remaining ingredients and season to taste.

Spoon into a serving bowl, cover with cling film and chill before serving with crudités or a selection of crisps.

260 LIPTOI

Preparation time:
5 minutes, plus
chilling

Serves 12

Calories:
176 per portion

YOU WILL NEED:
225 g/8 oz curd cheese
225 g/8 oz butter
½ teaspoon paprika
½ teaspoon caraway seeds
½ small onion, grated

Put all the ingredients in a bowl and beat thoroughly. Taste and add more paprika and caraway seeds if liked. Chill for at least 2 hours.

Serve with small savoury biscuits.

■ COOK'S TIP

Ideally you should use homemade mayonnaise for this dip. If this is impossible, choose a good quality prepared mayonnaise made with wine vinegar. Check the ingredients in the mayonnaise on the label.

■ COOK'S TIP

An alternative way to serve this cheese spread is to form the mixture into a loaf shape. Press pretzel biscuits into the sides and sprinkle paprika on top.

261 TEQUILA SUNRISE

Preparation time:
2 minutes

Serves 1

Calories: 236

YOU WILL NEED:
5 tablespoons tequila
175 ml/6 fl oz orange juice
1½ tablespoons grenadine

Mix the tequila and orange juice with some ice cubes in a shaker or jug and strain into a tall tumbler. Add the ice cubes and slowly pour in the grenadine.

Allow to settle, but stir once before drinking.

262 SALTY DOG

Preparation time:
2 minutes

Serves 1

Calories: 50

YOU WILL NEED:
1 tablespoon vodka
*1 tablespoon unsweetened grapefruit
  juice*
egg white
table salt
ice cubes, to serve

Measure the vodka and grapefruit juice into a jug and stir well. Lightly whisk a little egg white and pour on to a plate. Pour some salt on another plate. Dip the rim of the glass first in the egg white, then in the salt. Half-fill the glass with ice and pour over the cocktail.

■ COOK'S TIP

When mixing any cocktail it is important to get the proportions right, so always use the same item for measuring each ingredient – for example, an egg cup. If *you make cocktails frequently it is worth buying a standard measure called a 'jigger' which holds 45 ml/3 tablespoons.*

■ COOK'S TIP

Always use large ice cubes for serving in drinks. Never use small ones as these melt more quickly and dilute the drink. Prepare plenty of ice cubes in advance.

263 TOM COLLINS

Preparation time:
2 minutes

Serves 1

Calories: 116

YOU WILL NEED:
juice of ½ lemon
1½ teaspoons caster sugar
6 tablespoons gin
soda water to top up

Shake the ingredients well with ice and strain into a tall tumbler. Add some ice cubes and a good dash of soda water.

Decorate with lemon slices and cocktail cherries.

264 ANITA

Preparation time:
2 minutes

Serves 1

Calories: 46

YOU WILL NEED:
3 tablespoons orange juice
3 tablespoons lemon juice
3 dashes of Angostura bitters
soda water to top up

Shake the ingredients well with ice. Strain into a tumbler and top up with soda water.

Decorate with lemon and orange slices. Serve with a straw.

■ COOK'S TIP

Decorations for cocktails range from stuffed olives and maraschino cherries to slices of fresh fruit and sprigs of different herbs such as mint or borage.

Always spear cherries and large slices of fruit such as pineapple on cocktail sticks or small decorative skewers.

■ COOK'S TIP

At least one non-alcoholic drink is essential at parties now people are so aware of the dangers of drinking and driving.

PARTY PLANNING

It is important to plan a party that is well within your resources, your budget and the size of your home. It is essential to plan a menu that allows you to do most of the cooking and food presentation well in advance. Soups and pâtés are good starters to prepare ahead and chill (or freeze well ahead). Puddings and desserts like fruit compotes, mousses, chilled soufflés, ice creams and meringue-based desserts are also ideal for forward planning.

CATERING FOR LARGE NUMBERS

Forty people at a buffet will not eat ten times as much as four people at a dinner party. If, for example, you choose a dish which, when cooked for four or six, allows 225 g/8 oz of boned meat per portion, for a large party you can confidently reduce this to 150 g/5 oz per person. In any case it is never advisable to prepare any recipe in more than times-four the original. Take special care when you are multiplying dishes which have significant amounts of herbs and spices. On no account increase the amount of hot spices in direct proportion to the main ingredients. Add a little, taste the sauce and if necessary add a little more.

CHOOSING FISH

Always buy fish on the day it is to be cooked. Choose fish that has bright shiny eyes and a plump, firm body. The scales and skin should be shiny and moist. The smell of the fish is an excellent guide to the freshness. It should smell slightly sweet, certainly not unpleasant nor too fishy. Allow 175 g/6 oz fish without bones, 1 large or 2 small fillets per person.

CHOOSING POULTRY AND GAME

When buying poultry, the larger the bird, the better the value as the proportion of meat to bone is higher. Make sure you are given the giblets which make an excellent stock.

When cooking poultry that has been frozen make sure it is fully thawed first. Salmonella, a common cause of food poisoning, can lurk in the intestines of all birds, and is normally destroyed by heat. The body cavity, however, is more insulated by the surrounding flesh, and if this is still frozen, the heat may not penetrate enough to destroy the bacteria. It is very important to cool down a bird as quickly as possible and then chill it until needed.

There are several types of **chicken**:
POUSSINS are very small chickens weighing from 350-900 g/¾-2 lb) each. The larger ones are served one per portion, but the really tiny ones may need to be served in pairs.
BROILERS are smallish birds, usually about 12 weeks old, and are most often sold ready frozen. They weigh from 1.25-

1.5 kg (2½-3 lb). One bird should serve 3-4.
SPRING CHICKENS are small broilers, from 6-8 weeks old, and weighing about 900 g/2 lb. They can be cooked in a variety of ways, and will serve 2-3.
LARGE ROASTERS are aged about 10-15 weeks, and vary in size from 1.75-2.25 kg/4-5 lb and should serve 5-6 portions.

True CAPONS are no longer produced. The specially fattened birds available now are 'capon-style' chickens, with a good flavour and tender flesh. They usually weigh 3.5-4.5 kg/8-10 lb and serve 10.

Turkey is available all year round, ranging from mini birds of around 2.25 kg/5 lb to very large ones of 13.5 kg/30 lb. An average domestic cooker can handle a turkey of about 10.5 kg/23 lb, but not much more. Always buy the giblets with a whole bird. When stuffing a turkey, stuff only the neck of the bird and not the body cavity. If the cavity is stuffed, it may mean that the turkey has to be really overcooked to ensure that the stuffing itself is cooked.

As there is always very much less flesh on a **duck** than might appear, any bird that is less than 1.5 kg/3 lb in weight is not a good buy for it is likely to be mostly bone. An average duck weighs around 1.75-2.15 kg/4-5 lb and will not feed more than 4 people. A duck should be young with soft pliable feet, not rough or tough, and the feet and bill should be yellow; a dark orange indicates age.

Goose is a large bony bird with a very poor flesh to body size ratio. The flesh, though, has a very fine flavour and texture. Goose is very fatty and should always be pricked all over with a skewer and then stood on a rack to cook. An oven-ready goose should weigh about 4.5 kg/10 lb and will feed 6-8 people only. The bird must be young, preferably under 6 months old, with soft yellow feet, a yellow bill and yellowish fat.

Game is mainly available fresh. It is always hung in feather or fur (apart from venison), and undrawn for birds and hares. Hanging is essential to help to tenderize the meat and improve the characteristic flavour associated with game. The length of time required for the hanging varies greatly. Birds are usually ready when one of the tail feathers can be plucked out quite easily.

GROUSE will usually serve only one person, as will PARTRIDGE. PHEASANTS are often available – and cheaper – by the brace, meaning a cock and a hen. The cock is larger, with brightly coloured plumage, while the dull brown hen is plumper and more succulent. Pheasant should be hung for at least 3 days for a good flavour to develop, but it can be as long as 3 weeks if the weather is exceptionally cold. One pheasant will serve 2-3 people when roasted, and larger mature birds may serve up to 4 when casseroled with other ingredients. If plump and young, 1 PIGEON will serve one person; 2 squabs (fledglings) are needed per portion, and an older larger bird will serve 2 portions if casseroled with other ingredients. As QUAILS are so small, 2 can be served for a good portion, but 1 is usually enough. All WILD DUCK have very dry flesh because they are virtually fat-free. When they are roasted, they should be covered liberally with fat to prevent them drying out. A mallard or large wild duck should serve 2 people.

CHOOSING MEAT

When choosing **beef**, the lean of the meat should be bright to dark red with the fat a creamy white. Small flecks of fat should be visible throughout the lean. Flesh that has a dark red colour indicates that the carcass has been well hung, essential if the meat is to have a good flavour, and be very tender. Bright red meat often indicates that it is very fresh and unhung or not hung long enough for the flavour to develop properly. For beef on the bone allow 225-350 g/8-12 oz raw per person, plus a little extra for some to serve cold. For boned and rolled beef allow about 175 g/6 oz raw per person, plus a little extra. For steaks allow 150-175 g/5-6 oz raw per portion.

When choosing **lamb**, for leg, loin, shoulder and best end of neck on the bone, allow 350 g/12 oz raw per portion, with perhaps a little more for the loin and best end joints, plus extra to serve cold. For boned leg, loin, shoulder and best end of neck, which are rolled (before adding any stuffing), allow 175-225 g/6-8 oz raw per portion, plus extra to serve cold. For chops and cutlets, allow 1-2 per portion, depending on size, but 1 double loin or chump chop should be sufficient. With noisettes, again allow 1-2 depending on size.

When selecting a joint of **pork**, look for a good layer of firm white fat with a thinnish elastic skin around the pale pink, smooth and fine-grained lean. A roasting joint should have a good rind that can be scored to give a good crackling when cooked – the butcher should do this. Remember that pork must always be thoroughly cooked.

For pork joints on the bone, allow 225-350 g/8-12 oz per portion, plus extra to serve cold. For boned and rolled joints allow about 175 g/6 oz per portion; allow a little less than this for tenderloin. For pork chops, allow 1 per person, but for small cutlets and boneless pork slices, you may need to allow 2.

Veal is the meat from a very young calf; the flesh should be a very light pink in colour, and soft and moist with only very little fat which should be firm and either white or faintly pink. Do not buy veal that is over-flabby and really wet looking. If veal looks dry, brownish, or has a very mottled appearance, it is stale.

For veal roasting joints on the bone, allow 225-350 g/8-12 oz raw per portion. For roasting joints, boned and rolled, allow 175-225 g/6-8 oz raw per portion, plus extra to serve cold. For fillets or escalopes (boneless) allow 100-150 g/4-5 oz raw per portion. For chops allow 1 veal chop taken from the loin; or 1-2 cutlets taken from the neck end or top of loin, depending on the size of the animal.

CHOOSING CHEESE

Offer a choice of 4-6 cheeses including a blue cheese and a goat's cheese at a dinner party.

Avoid any cheese that looks dry, sweaty or has blue mould on the surface. When choosing soft cheeses, such as Brie and Camembert, press the top surface lightly with the fingertips. The cheese should yield slightly. It should be creamy in texture throughout, without any chalkiness in the centre. This chalkiness means that the cheese has not been ripened sufficiently and will remain in this condition. Goat's milk cheeses should be consumed on the day they are purchased, as the flavour soon becomes 'soapy'.

Ideally, cheese should be stored in a cool, draught-proof larder – the refrigerator is the next best place. Cheese should be removed from the refrigerator and un-wrapped at least 1 hour before it is required so that it has time to come to room temperature.

APERITIFS AND DIGESTIFS

The function of an aperitif is to freshen the palate, without being so heavy that it dulls the appetite. Sherry of all types is a good choice. As a general rule, the 'drier' the wine, the more important it is to serve it well chilled. Wine-based aperitifs may be served 'straight', chilled and undiluted; 'on the rocks', which means poured over cracked ice; or diluted with a mixer such as soda water or tonic water. For many people Champagne is the most festive of all aperitifs. You should get 6-7 glasses from a standard (75 cl) bottle.

For cocktails you will need gin, vodka and white rum, all excellent mixers that form the base of hundreds of recipes. Purists recommend serving Scotch whisky neat, or simply with water so that the true flavour of the grain is enjoyed, but it may also be served, with or without ice cubes, with soda water, dry ginger, ginger wine, or as a cocktail.

As an after-dinner drink, or digestif, a good French brandy, either Cognac or Armagnac, is a popular choice. Port, another traditional after-dinner drink, is one of the world's finest fortified wines. Liqueurs offer a bewildering range of after-dinner drinks. They are all spirit-based and vary in strength from about 30° to a powerful 55°.

Generally speaking, all wines benefit to some extent from 'laying down' or storing. This applies particularly to fine clarets and red or white burgundies, some of the best red wines from Italy, Spain, California and South America, and white wines from Bordeaux and the sweeter dessert varieties from Germany. The lighter red wines and light, dry, fruity white wines are really meant to be enjoyed 'young' and do not improve so much with keeping. The ideal conditions are a cellar, a dark cupboard or the space under the stairs, which is constantly cool – experts advise a temperature of around 10°C/50°F. All wine in corked bottles should be stored horizontally, so that the liquid is in contact with the cork. This prevents the cork from drying out and allowing air to enter the bottle.

Fine wines should be handled with care. Remove the bottles gently from the rack and slowly raise them to the upright position. If the wine has matured in the bottle, a small, flaky deposit, or 'sediment', will have formed. As you gently pour the wine the deposit will remain in the 'punt', the indentation at the base of the bottle. Only the finest clarets, burgundies and port need to be decanted, to be sure of separating the wine from the deposit, but of course you may pour any wine into a decanter to serve it.

Perhaps the most important factor affecting the serving of wine is temperature. Nearly all wines have a temperature band of (at most) 4°C/39°F at which they will taste at their best, and the difference between a wine served at its ideal temperature and one served degrees too warm or cold can be startling. A simple way of checking the wine is at the right temperature is to leave it somewhere which is already at the temperature required, for 2-3 hours.

To enjoy a really fine wine to the full, serve it in plain uncoloured glasses that are only half filled.

IDEAL SERVING TEMPERATURE

16°-19°C/ 61°-55°F	Mature red wines, Rhône reds, northern Italian reds, Californian and Australian reds
14°-16°C/ 56°-61°F	Young red wines, Chianti, Rioja, Port, Madeira
12°-14°C/ 53°-56°F	Light red wine (Beaujolais, Valpolicella), medium and sweet sherry, white port, best white Burgundy
9°-12°C/ 58°-53°F	All other white and rosé wine. Dry sherry, Champagne
5°-9°C/ 40°-48°F	Other sparkling wines. All sweet white wines.

EXAMPLES OF DIFFERENT WINES

Light red wines: Beaujolais; Chinon; Mâcon rouge; Bardolino; Lambrusco; Valpolicella; New Zealand red wines

Medium red wines: Beaune; Côtes du Rhône; Medoc; Barbaresco; Chianti; Rioja; Rioja Reserva; top Californian and Australian Cabernet Sauvignon red wines

Full-bodied red wines: Bordeaux *crus classés*; Bourgogne domaine-bottled wines; Chateauneuf-du-Pape; Hermitage; Barolo; Dão; Australian Shiraz; Californian Zinfandel

Light dry white wines: Alsace Sylvaner; Gaillac; Muscadet; Pouilly-fumé; Sancerre; Saumur; Sauvignon; Frascati; Vinho Verde

Full dry white wines: Bourgogne blanc; Chablis; Chardonnay; Graves; Riesling d'Alsace; Soave; Verdicchio; white Rioja

Medium sweet white wines: Anjou blanc; Vouvray; most German white wines; Orvieto abboccato; many English wines

Sweet white wines: Barsac; Monbazillac; Sauternes; Auslese or Beerenauslese; most Muscat wines

Rosé wines: Rosé d'Anjou, Rosé de Provence; Tavel; Mateus rosé

Sparkling wines: Blanquette de Limoux; Champagne; Clairette de Die; Crémant; Asti Spumante; Lambrusco

---

WINE AND FOOD CHART

Good match = one glass; Excellent match = two glasses

WINE	Soups	Pâtés and starters	Pasta	Seafood	Fish	Savoury flans	Poultry and meat	Red meat	Game	Desserts	Cheeses
Light red wine		Good	Excellent			Good	Excellent				Good
Medium red wine			Good				Good	Excellent			Excellent
Full-bodied red wine			Good				Excellent	Excellent	Excellent		Good
Light dry white wine			Good	Excellent							
Full dry white wine		Good			Excellent	Good	Excellent				Good
Medium sweet white wine	Good	Good			Good	Good	Good				
Sweet white wine										Excellent	
Rosé wine		Good	Good			Good	Good				
Sparkling wines			Good	Good	Excellent		Good			Good	

MENU SUGGESTIONS

ELEGANT DINNER PARTY FOR 6

Prawn pâté (recipe 8)
Duck Breasts with Horseradish Sauce
(recipe 25)
with a summer green salad with Honey
and Lemon Dressing (recipe 13)
Rose Petal Tart (recipe 45)

Serve a medium red wine with the duck

BUFFET SUPPER FOR 30

Vol au Vents (recipe 162)
Mexican Dip with Crudités (recipe 169)
Pilaff (recipe 172)
Chilli Chicken Drumsticks (recipe 174)
Quiche Provencale (recipe 177 – make 2)
Tomato and Feta Cheese Salad
(recipe 182 × 2)
Chocolate Brandy Gateau (recipe 188)
selection of cheeses

serve crisp dry white and light red wines

SUPPER PARTY FOR 4

Fennel Soup with Garlic Croûtons
(recipe 55 × 2)
Fettucine in Four Cheeses (recipe 73)
Tomato and Leek Salad (recipe 79)
Nectarines in Grand Marnier (recipe 88)

Serve a medium red wine with the pasta

BARBECUE LUNCH FOR 6-8

Barbecued Boned Leg of Lamb (recipe 89)
with Creole Sauce (recipe 122)
Winchester Sausages (recipe 98)
Seafood Kebabs (recipe 111)
Pepper, Anchovy and Tomato Salad
(recipe 117 × 2)
Red Salad (recipe 119)
Iced Lemon Rice Pudding (recipe 125)
Grapefruit and Mint Ice Cream
(recipe 128)

*Serve chilled dry white wine, cold lager or
chilled lemonade (recipe 209)*

DISCO PARTY SUPPER FOR 15-20 TEENAGERS

Potato Skins with Soured Cream
(recipe 243)
Turkey Bites with Tomato Dip
(recipe 196)
Cheese and Onion Quiche (recipe 197)
Moussaka (recipe 204)
Chinese Cabbage Salad (recipe 205)
Banana Ice Cream (recipe 207)
Cinnamon Cheesecake with Kiwi Fruit
(recipe 83)

*serve jugs of Lemonade (recipe 209) or
Anita (recipe 264)*

VEGETARIAN LUNCH FOR 4

Leeks in Pastry Cases (recipe 2)
or
Melitzano Salata (recipe 36)
Savoury Roulade (recipe 176)
with Green salad (recipe 184)
Melon and Raspberries in Sauternes
(recipe 47)

*Serve a light dry white wine with the
roulade*

SUMMER WEDDING LUNCH FOR 12

Quail's Eggs in Vermouth Jelly
(recipe 145)
Coulibiac (recipe 142)
Lime Mousse (recipe 143)

*serve Champagne or Champagne
Cocktails (recipe 144)*

COCKTAIL PARTY FOOD FOR 30

Tuna and Parmesan Puffs (recipe 244)
Parma Ham Nibbles (recipe 245)
Smoked Salmon and Cress Pinwheels
(recipe 247)
Devilled Dip (recipe 259)
Chive Biscuits with Sage Cream
(recipe 254)
Japanese Almonds (recipe 246)

INDEX